THE ELLEMENTS OF PERSONAL STYLE

{ 25 MODERN FASHION ICONS ON HOW TO DRESS, SHOP, AND LIVE }

THE ELLEMENTS OF PERSONAL STYLE

{ 25 MODERN FASHION ICONS ON HOW TO DRESS, SHOP, AND LIVE }

By ELLE EDITORS *JOE ZEE* & *MAGGIE BULLOCK*
FOREWORD BY *ROBERTA MYERS*
PHOTOGRAPHY BY *THOMAS WHITESIDE*
WITH *ALEXA BRAZILIAN*

GOTHAM BOOKS   MELCHER MEDIA

Gotham Books Published by Penguin Group (USA) Inc.; 375 Hudson St., New York, New York 10014, U.S.A. Penguin Group (Canada), 90 Eglinton Avenue East, Suite 700, Toronto, Ontario M4P 2Y3, Canada (a division of Pearson Penguin Canada Inc); Penguin Books Ltd, 80 Strand, London WC2R ORL, England; Penguin Ireland, 25 St. Stephen's Green, Dublin 2, Ireland (a division of Penguin Books Ltd); Penguin Group (Australia), 250 Camberwell Road, Camberwell, Victoria 3124, Australia (a division of Pearson Australia Group Pty Ltd); Penguin Books India Pvt Ltd, 11 Community Centre, Panchsheel Park, New Delhi—110 017, India; Penguin Group (NZ), 67 Apollo Drive, Rosedale, North Shore 0632, New Zealand (a division of Pearson New Zealand Ltd); Penguin Books (South Africa) (Pty) Ltd, 24 Sturdee Avenue, Rosebank, Johannesburg 2196, South Africa; Penguin Books Ltd, Registered Offices: 80 Strand, London WC2R ORL, England

PUBLISHED BY GOTHAM BOOKS, A MEMBER OF PENGUIN GROUP (USA) INC.

Gotham Books and the skyscraper logo are trademarks of Penguin Group (USA) Inc.
First Printing, October 2010

10 9 8 7 6 5 4 3 2 1
978-1-592-40567-1
Printed in China

© 2010 Hachette Filipacchi Media U.S., Inc.

DESIGN BY PAUL RITTER

THANK YOU

To the women who opened up their closets, homes, and lives for this book: Lea Michele, Erin Wasson, Padma Lakshmi, Fergie, Anjelica Huston, Ashley Greene, Tracee Ellis Ross, Christina Hendricks, Diane von Furstenberg, Olivia Wilde, Estelle, Yvonne Force Villareal, Margherita Missoni, Katherine Pope, Dita Von Teese, Kate Mara, Alicia Keys, Becki Newton, Candace Bushnell, Janie Bryant, Charlotte Gainsbourg, Fatima Robinson, Minnie Mortimer, Charlotte Rampling, and Milla Jovovich.

To Gotham Books, especially Bill Shinker and Lauren Marino, for believing in this book and providing it with a wonderful home. To the brilliant ELLE team, including Paul Ritter, Alexis Bryan Morgan, Sara Culley, Ellyn Chestnut, Joann Pailey, Kate Lanphear, Candice Rainy, Kate Davidson Hudson, Jade Frampton, Kyle Anderson, Jennifer Gach, Jodi Belden, Kristen Shirley, Mitsu Tsuchiya, Jennifer Weisel, Alexa Brazilian, Rachel Rosenblit, Seth Plattner, Julie Vadnal, Jacqueline Bates, Thomas Whiteside, Annie Ladino, Juliet Jernigan, Liz Hodges, Keith Pollock, Katherine Daniels, Malina Joseph, Dorothee Walliser, Lauren Kirk, Sandy Destruge, Yashua Simmons, Marina Lange, Jade Lopez, Julianne Klempf, Molly Destruge, Woldy Reyes, Michelle Goodman, Stephanie Fairyington, Shirley J. Velasquez, Corrie Pikul, Brendan Cummings, and Laura Cantekin.

And to the people who helped make every shoot and interview run smoothly, including Tara Friedlander, Melanie Inglessis, Mark Townsend, Estee Stanley, Josh Goldfarb, Kevin Ryan, Rachel at Art and Commerce, Maud, Kristin at Community, Hillary Siskind, Sean Patterson, Laura Lightbody, Sarah Daniella, Jason Medina, Ronit Shapow, Veronica Rodriguez, Chris Psaila, Christina Papadopolos, Raina Seides, Tucker Gurley, Nick Barose, Jutta Weiss, Jaclyn Bashoff, David Babaii, Lisa Jachno, Davy Kirk, Vanessa Scali, Rebecca Yerkovich, Scott Williams, Sarah Ault, Kerry Malouf, India at Photogenics, Holly Shakoor, Lawren Sample, Philip Carreon, Rachel Goodwin, Emese Szenasy, Alixe Boyer, Kate Bartle, Elizabeth Luby, Heidi Crow, Maria Herrera, Karla, Charles Dujic, Spencer Barnes, Alyssa at Solo, Cara Donatto, A.J. Crimson, Dickey for Hair Rules, Dante Blandshaw, Conrad Dornan, Tracy Alfajora, Joe Management, Maddy Aspes, Luca Lassaro, Silvana Belli, John Huynh, Priscilla Porianda, Jessica Tingley, Jerrllyn Stephens, Victoria Bell, Andrea Martin, Coleen Campbell Otwel, Stephen Lewis, Renee Geist, Cynthia Alvarez, Ashunta Sheriff, Krystal at Epiphany, Ruth Bernstein, Haley Urman, Chris McMillan, Jamie Greenberg, Patti at Solo, Dana and Crosby at The Wall Group, Heather Schroder, Maureen at Eastern Talent, Ashlee Barnes, Tiger, Terry Saxon, Julien Edoardo, Tatsu Yamanaka, Jed Root, Vanessa and Federica at Jed Root, Nathalie Canguilhem, Craig Schneider, Paige Bingham, Khadijah Myers, Jo Baker, Denise Vizcarra, Julianne Kaye, Cyril Laloue, Steven Canavan, Chris Brenner, Jake Bailey, Mara Roszak, Sumer Fawaz, Angelica Gleason, Tyler Whiteside, Linda Whiteside, Devon Jarvis, Mark Platt, Eddy Alcantara, and Devin Doyle.

Melcher Media would also like to thank Eric Baum, David E. Brown, Amelie Cherlin, Ben Gibson, Barbara Gogan, Melissa Goldstein, Gigi Gray, Coco Joly, Kenyatta Matthews, Myles McDonnell, Naomi Mizusaki, Tracy Morford, Minju Pak, Tricia Patterson, Katherine Raymond, Lia Ronnen, Jessi Rymill, Julia Sourkoff, Alex Tart, Kara Taylor, Rebecca Wiener, and Megan Worman.

PRODUCED BY MELCHER MEDIA, INC.

124 W. 13th Street, New York, NY 10011 www.melcher.com

Charles Melcher, President; Bonnie Eldon, Associate Publisher; Duncan Bock, Editor in Chief;
Holly Rothman, Senior Editor;
Shoshana Thaler and Lauren Nathan, Associate Editors;
Daniel Del Valle, Production Associate; Kurt Andrews, Production Director

To the brilliant and creative staff of ELLE

CONTENTS

FOREWORD BY *ROBERTA MYERS* page 8

LEA MICHELE page 12

ERIN WASSON page 20

PADMA LAKSHMI page 32

FERGIE page 44

ANJELICA HUSTON page 54

ASHLEY GREENE page 66

TRACEE ELLIS ROSS page 72

CHRISTINA HENDRICKS page 82

DIANE VON FURSTENBERG page 90

OLIVIA WILDE page 100

ESTELLE page 108

YVONNE FORCE VILLAREAL page 116

MARGHERITA MISSONI page 126

KATHERINE POPE page 138

DITA VON TEESE page 146

KATE MARA page 158

ALICIA KEYS page 164

BECKI NEWTON page 170

CANDACE BUSHNELL page 182

JANIE BRYANT page 190

CHARLOTTE GAINSBOURG page 200

FATIMA ROBINSON page 212

MINNIE MORTIMER page 222

CHARLOTTE RAMPLING page 232

MILLA JOVOVICH page 244

PHOTOGRAPHY CREDITS page 256

n 1945, when Russian émigré Hélène Lazareff, who'd recently returned to Paris after several years as a journalist in New York, launched the first edition of ELLE in France, it was with an elegantly simple—and subversive—mission: to "open women's appetites." In a city that had been ravaged by war and in a country that had been duty- and class-bound for centuries, it was an extraordinarily bold move: a magazine created by a woman and run by one that didn't aim to tell its readers what to do, but would instead help them figure out what they wanted. Its influence was enormous: ELLE democratized fashion, ushering in a way for the masses to both consume and transmit what was once the exclusive province of the aristocracy. As one wealthy reader said to Lazareff: "It's almost criminal the way your magazine is breaking down traditions. You can no longer tell the difference between my maid, my neighbor, and myself."

When Lazareff counseled her readers that the best way to dress during the cold of winter was to wear pants (an activity that had once been illegal in France), she sparked a postwar fashion trend, freeing working women everywhere from the physically (and psychologically) limiting uniform of stockings and skirts. But ELLE wasn't simply a fashion magazine; it became the cultural bellwether for all French women, a distinctly female voice on the issues of the day. Lazareff published the work of Simone de Beauvoir and Colette, discovered Brigitte Bardot, and wrote freely about the rights of women to not just participate in French intellectual life, but to lead it. Sixty-five years later, ELLE is such a part of the French way of living that nearly every woman in the country is said to have read it.

It was a magazine for modern women—a message and an idea that has translated so well that ELLE is now published around the globe. With 42 editions in more than 60 countries and 23 million readers, ELLE is the world's No. 1 fashion magazine. ELLE's first "foreign edition" was ELLE U.S., launched monthly in 1985 by legendary French publication director Regis Pagniez, who was the architect of the magazine's iconic look: sumptuous photographs on luxurious oversize pages that were saturated with richly hued, eye-popping color. Its first cover featured the dark-eyed, dark-haired beauty Yasmin Le Bon, who was regularly shot by the equally legendary ELLE photographer Gilles Bensimon. Since its inception, ELLE has challenged the notion of what "American beauty" can be, championing a look that went far beyond the normative fair-skinned, fair-haired models favored at the time. ELLE's launch was an unqualified hit and forever changed the landscape of American fashion magazines.

Twenty-five years later, we celebrate that launch with another: a book about personal style, a concept central to ELLE's DNA from the beginning.

ELLE was the first fashion magazine to display any sustained interest in popular culture and the nexus where high fashion—designer fashion from New York, Paris, and Milan—and the street, i.e., how real women dress, meet. But more important, ELLE mixed the very American idea of sartorial freedom with the French notion that fashion was something cultured women could know about and consume without being seen as frivolous. That fashion was, in fact, to be integrated into a woman's daily wardrobe according to her own tastes and comfort level. Out of that grew ELLE's unique and thoroughly modern message: Fashion—literally, that which is current—should always be subordinate to style, the very personal and profound message that a woman sends to the world about herself. Style, of course, isn't merely expressed in the way a woman dresses; it's about everything, from the way she lives (from architecture to table settings), to where she travels, to her taste in music, art, food, cars, technology. In short, life.

At ELLE, there is no house style or aesthetic, but there is an ethos: We are the modern fashion magazine. Modernist architect Mies van der Rohe famously said: "God is in the details." For ELLE, personal style can be found in the exact same place. Personal style is just that: personal. A million little details that add up to a "look." The 25 women in this book exemplify the idea that developing a strong personal style can help you feel more powerful in the world and more comfortable in your skin. It can also be a lot of fun. These 25 modern women gave us enormous access: to their homes, their closets, and their histories. They show us just how they developed their unique and expressive styles. They have a lot to teach us all about pushing past our comfort zones (and our lazy habits) and feeling confident with our choices, helping us to expand our ideas of not just how we look, but who we can become.

At ELLE we've become more than just a magazine, and our recent history has brought a renewed energy and look to the brand across many media. The 2007 appointments of Creative Director Joe Zee, who cast and styled the 25 women, and Design Director Paul Ritter, who oversaw the book's design, and the 2005 appointment of then Senior Writer and current Deputy Editor Maggie Bullock, who interviewed and poked and prodded her subjects for their secrets to looking so fabulous, have been instrumental in our success and in helping shape what ELLE will be in the future.

I thank all of them, who worked tirelessly on this project, as well as photographer Thomas Whiteside and Fashion News Editor Alexa Brazilian, and the whole ELLE staff for their contributions to this, ELLE U.S.'s first book. And, of course, the 25 amazing women whose ELLEments of style inspire us all.

MICHELE, PHOTOGRAPHED
IN LOS ANGELES AT THE HOME
OF HER STYLIST ESTEE STANLEY,
IN THE OSCAR DE LA RENTA
GOWN SHE WORE TO THE 2010
GOLDEN GLOBES. *GLEE* WON
FOR BEST TELEVISION SERIES.

Opposite: A four-year-old Michele on
Christmas morning

Lea Michele

LEA MICHELE
RED-CARPET EVOLVER

OCCUPATION	*Actress, singer*
BEST KNOWN FOR	*Belting out tunes on Broadway and TV's* Glee
HOME BASE	*West Hollywood, Los Angeles*

Michele has committed to memory Barbra's Fanny Brice, the poignant, sometimes bumbling would-be performer—sound familiar?—from *Funny Girl.* "I love love, and Fanny loves love; she loves performing, and I'm very much like that," Michele says. "You've got your Holly Golightlys, and then you've got your Fanny Brices. I'm a Fanny Brice."

After three years in *Les Miz,* she was cast in the original Broadway production of *Ragtime.* But at 14, she left Broadway for Tenafly High in search of "that 'normal' thing everybody talks about," she says. "To be honest, it wasn't that enjoyable."

In her senior year, she returned to work in *Fiddler on the Roof,* eventually turning down a spot at New York University to stay onstage. It was the rock musical *Spring Awakening,* a show that shocked audiences with aggressive melodies and explicit adolescent sexuality—tackling nudity, masturbation, rape, and abortion, among other thorny subjects—that lit her career on fire. Michele had originated Wendla, the show's ultranaive female lead, at 14, when the script was still being workshopped. Six years later, Wendla made her a bona fide Broadway star.

Still, when she left *Spring Awakening* in 2008, agents and casting directors

T'S ALMOST TOO EASY to draw parallels between actress and singer Lea Michele and Rachel Berry, the show-tune-belting teen she plays on *Glee,* Fox's phenomenally successful dark comedy about musical outcasts in an all-American high school. Rachel possesses enough go-get-'em chutzpah to fuel the whole glee club, if not the entire state of Ohio (where the show is set). Michele is a former Broadway baby who, upon landing a role in *Les Misérables* at the age of eight, realized "that I could never and would never want to do anything else," she says.

Michele's Rachel is a uniquely endearing striver, equal parts grating overachiever and sweet social nincompoop; one of those kids who find their purpose in life before most of us learn to tie our shoes. "Rachel just needs her stage," Michele says. "When I was younger, I was outgoing and open and loud, like her. Now, I guess I'm able to let that out on the stage, so in real life I toned down a little bit."

Truth is, at 24 Michele's real life exceeds the wildest imaginings of Rachel Berry—or, indeed, of Lea Michele Sarfati, as she's known back home in Tenafly, New Jersey. A gregarious, high-energy kid, Michele wasn't one to idolize the pop princesses of her generation. She grew up mimicking hilarious, less-than-perfect comediennes: Fran Drescher, Gilda Radner, Cheri Oteri.

On Barbra Streisand: "She's this sort of godlike creature in my head."

Opposite: "I had picked this long, beautiful white Chloé dress to wear to the Grammys, but at the last minute we realized it was see-through!"

Michele's patron saint, Barbra Streisand, seen here in *Funny Girl*

At six, on a family trip to NYC's Harleywood

"BY NO MEANS AM I A FAKE PERSON. I'M FROM NEW YORK— WE DON'T PRETEND TO BE ANYTHING OTHER THAN WHO WE ARE."

— LEA

"were a little hesitant to take the first bite," says Michele. She was told, Fanny Brice-style, that she just wasn't cut out for TV. "I was never pretty enough to play the pretty girl, and I was never quirky enough to play the quirky girl," she says. "They didn't know where to put me." One agent sent her to audition for the role of a 25- to 35-year-old district attorney on *Law & Order*. If you've seen *Glee*, you know that was a mistake. "I was 20, looking 15, and I'd been playing a 14-year-old on Broadway," she says. "It didn't fit."

Glee, of course, fits like a glove. (Indeed, the show's creator, Ryan Murphy, has said that he wrote Michele's part after meeting her during one of her auditioning trips to L.A.) In a matter of months, the show propelled her into the national spotlight, where she has already demonstrated a certain natural aptitude for the high-stakes fashion merry-go-round of awards ceremonies and red carpets. Still a relative novice, she makes smart, confident choices: a feather-skirted navy cocktail dress for the Grammys, a peacock green Catherine Malandrino gown with a plunging neckline for the Screen Actors Guild Awards, and a rainbow of other well-cut, relatively unfettered frocks that tend to show off what she considers her best asset: her legs.

In fashion, Michele takes calculated risks and, more important, goes with her gut. For instance, the sweeping black Oscar de la Renta gown she wore to her first Golden Globes (and again for this *ELLEments* shoot) defied the prevailing wisdom—and Murphy's express instructions—that serious, somewhat stolid black is not the way young

"I'm very into taking care of my body, eating clean, doing morning yoga on my rooftop, and running in the canyons. I need to be strong for the crazy dance numbers in *Glee*."
Right: In a Hervé L. Leroux gown

starlets make their first major fashion splash. Hollywood stylist Estee Stanley (the head of Michele's glam squad and the owner of the to-die-for house she's photographed in here) had dutifully stocked up on bright, appropriately youthful dresses, but as soon as Michele spotted the de la Renta hanging in Stanley's own closet, "I was like, 'I need this dress,'" she says. First she had to get Murphy to agree. "It was like I was Hodel in *Fiddler*, begging Tevye to accept her for marrying a non-Jew," she

says. "I was like, 'You *have* to accept this dress.'" Ultimately, everybody won: The dress charmed the fashion gawkers, and *Glee* took home its first Golden Globe. Post-afterparty, Michele and her boyfriend, actor Theo Stockman (of Broadway's *American Idiot*), ordered takeout from L.A. late-night haunt Jerry's Famous Deli, went home, climbed into bed—dress and all—and feasted on veggie clubs and French fries. "It was amazing," says Michele. And doubtless the first of many amazing nights.

INSPIRATION BOARD

15. When I fell in love I was wearing:

A skirt that I was told rescembled a "disco ball"

9. People compliment my: eyelashes.

They're very long. I have my dad to thank for them. People # always think they're fake.

1. My most prized possession: A ring from my grandpa

He took the stone from an old tie pin and made it into a ring for me. When I wear it I think of him, and in a fire thats what I would take w/ me.

On screen as Rachel Berry. "Rachel's very talented and driven, but she has the same insecurities any 15-year-old would."

MICHELE MASTERS PARTY CHIC WITH BODY CONFIDENCE AND AN EYE FOR KNOCK-'EM-DEAD DRESSES

Instead of jumping from look to look for each big event, as many young starlets do, Michele sticks to what she likes and, most important, what she looks good in—a feat typically mastered by only the most seasoned celebrities. The *Glee* girl looks for hot, saturated colors and always plays to her biggest strength: her legs. She jokes that if her stylist, Estee Stanley, hears her say, "Make this shorter!" one more time, "she's going to go crazy!"

HER FAVORITE SHOPS

CURRENT/ELLIOTT
currentelliott.com

LA ROK
larok.com

SWITCH
*238 South Beverly Drive
Beverly Hills, CA 90212
(310) 860-1650*

TOPSHOP
*us.topshop.com
478 Broadway
New York, NY 10012
Personal Shopping
Service: (212) 966-9455*

STYLE STUDY

A one-shouldered Grecian dress is one of Michele's go-to looks.

Jewel tones pop on-camera and complement her coloring.

This thigh-grazing cocktail number looks fresh and youthful with loose hair and minimal accessories.

Left and above: *Michele met her best friend, Jonathan Groff (Glee's Jesse St. James) when they costarred on Broadway in* Spring Awakening.

"As a child, I'd entertain my mom with imitations of Gilda Radner." Another hero: Celine Dion (below).

❝I TRY TO STAY AWAY FROM SUPERTIGHT DRESSES, BUT I LOVE SOMETHING LOW-CUT, AND, OF COURSE, IT'S ALWAYS GOT TO BE SHORT!❞

LEA

A girlish hue and layers of soft embellishment give this Isaac Mizrahi dress youthful innocence. Keep accessories simple—this dress is decoration enough.

ERIN WASSON

NEO-GRUNGE

OCCUPATION	*Model, stylist, designer*
BEST KNOWN FOR	*Sparking fashion trends*
HOME BASE	*East Village, New York City*

RIN WASSON'S CURLS are bothering her. "Too *pretty*," she says, sniffing at the word like an insult. She grabs her hair in her fists, yanking until it becomes something a little more unkempt—a little less "done." "Okay. Better," she says, smiling apologetically at the hairstylist whose work she's just made, well, way better.

Wasson's East Village loft looks like the kind of place where a leftover member of Jefferson Airplane might hole up, with a slouchy, wraparound couch that could sleep three; a well-used stack of vinyl; tapestry-hung walls; and various rough-hewn furnishings from the '60s and '70s. It's not the way one expects multimillionaire models to live, but then Wasson has never been one for the high-gloss side of her business. When she started out in the mid-'90s, she showed up to castings in baggy jeans, men's tank tops, and skater shoes, her head half shaved. The industry didn't know quite what to make of this sexy ragamuffin from Texas. "My agent was getting phone calls in the beginning like, 'Gosh, she really doesn't look polished!'" says Wasson with a laugh. "And in the end, this whole unpolished, undone, disheveled look has become my thing. It's ironic, to say the least."

To qualify as a "supermodel" is to be more than beautiful; you need to be "commercial"—i.e., relatably pretty enough to sell mascara to millions as the face of, say, Maybelline, as Wasson

does—and "editorial," i.e., interesting enough to propel fashion's collective imagination. "I can look weird and kooky if you need me to, but at the same time I'm still almost like the girl next door," says Wasson, whose appeal is also distinctly American: golden-skinned and dirty blond, athletic, outdoorsy, and also somehow utterly at home in French couture. She has modeled for J.Crew, Victoria's Secret, and H&M, but she didn't transcend fashion-world fame to become a pop-culture property—the kind who is regularly mobbed by teen girls with messy hair, dressed in eerily familiar cutoffs and oversize shirts—until 2007, when she discovered a neighbor in her apartment building, the then-fledgling designer Alexander Wang.

The two had a Siamese-twin fashion sense—often wearing the same uniform of ripped white tees and legging-tight black jeans—and they shared a certain idea of how women should dress. "Alex and I always thought, What's wrong with going to an event in shorts, tights, and high heels?" she says. "I've always thought that it's much more interesting to just sort of be the same person bleeding in from day into night. Why change your thing?" On one occasion, Wasson wore one of her day-to-night standbys, a pair of regulation gray sweatpants from Foot Locker with the legs rolled up, to one of Wang's after-parties. "Everybody was like, 'Oh my God, is she really wearing *sweatpants*?' Yeah, but I'm wearing six-inch heels with them," she says. "I'm a walking contradic-

Opposite: Wasson, wearing Dries Van Noten pants and a WTAPS shirt in front of a wall of sketches by artist/musician Daniel Johnston

> **"THE WHOLE 'MODEL OFF DUTY' LOOK IS HUMOROUS TO ME. I JUST DON'T THINK ABOUT IT LIKE THAT—YOU GET UP IN THE MORNING AND YOU GET DRESSED."**
>
> ERIN

tion." (The aforementioned taut-and-tawny beauty helps, too.)

When she styled two of Wang's early shows, the pair changed, seemingly overnight, the way fashion-y young girls wanted to dress. Wasson, who for so long had been frustrated by the idea that models were blank canvases to be seen and not heard, wanted to champion her models' own individuality. "Here's a business with all of these righteous women who come from corners of the world and have incredibly different stories and upbringings and personalities and hobbies," she says. Her style ethos: "You should embrace exactly who you are and exactly where you're from. Have your own perspective."

Her own perspective is deeply rooted in Irving, Texas. When her father entered her in a local newspaper's modeling contest, Wasson was a lanky 15-year-old, too busy traveling with her basketball team to bother reading fashion magazines. When the paper called to say she'd won, she didn't see her future open wide up; she thought the best part was a $1,000 shopping spree—"more money than I could have ever imagined"—with which she bought black-and-white wing-tipped Dr. Martens.

Texas, Wasson says, "is a denim-obsessed state." That's where she got into the habit of cutoff Levi's 501s from the thrift store and V-neck white Hanes tees from Walmart—still the basics of her wardrobe and the inspiration behind her own designs for her three-year-old jewelry collection, Low Luv,

and the capsule collection she designs for streetwear label RVCA. "On top of that, you add all your flair," explains Wasson, who wears an amalgam of long necklaces, vintage silver rings, turquoise, and rough-hewn stones. "Oh my God, I can never wear enough jewelry," she says. "If I could have three rings on every finger, I would be happy—they're going to say more about you than going out and buying something of the moment." Though she's

amassed mountains of designer gifts over the years—piles of Balenciaga, McQueen, and Chanel, and, of course, a lifetime supply of Alexander Wang—her most treasured possession is an old friend, a timeworn, holey black hoodie that she's had since she was 15. "I'm almost baffled by the fact that it's still in my possession," she says. "All the places it's been, the milestones it's been through with me. I'm like, 'Wow, and you're still here.'"

On her home decor philosophy: "I like to juxtapose total crap next to insane, talented beauty." *Right:* Wearing a tank from her own line and pants by Maria Cher, "an insane designer I discovered in Argentina"

ERIN'S WORLD

Wasson scavenged the cartoon heads when a friend was about to throw them away.

A chair by artist Robert Loughlin in front of a wood sculpture by Doyle Lane

Sectional corner couch adopted from a 2010 ELLE shoot

A low-key vanity for a low-key beauty; *left:* "In my apartment, people can't tell the difference between this really amazing artwork—the Daniel Johnstons, Fia Backströms—and the $20 piece of junk art."

In her trademark cutoffs and a vintage vest; *right:* Bags dot the back wall of her bedroom. *Below:* The sticker-covered front door

INSPIRATION BOARD

Classic 10-hole Dr. Martens, the kind of grunge-era standard Wasson helped bring back into fashion

Backstage at her fall 2010 runway show. Of her own look: "I wanted to channel Rod Stewart."

WASSON REGULARLY REAPPROPRIATES ATHLETIC GEAR AND STREET-WEAR STAPLES

"I just get up in the morning and get dressed. I don't think about it. If I'm feeling lazy, I'm going to wear sweatpants," says Wasson. To upgrade your own sweats, pair with high heels, a structured blazer, and one piece of statement jewelry—a cuff, a dangly earring—and a fearless attitude: Conviction is key!

Wasson shows her Texan pride—and an early flair for layering. Below right: Growing up, Wasson— seen here in high school— was "a total jock."

STYLE STUDY

Wasson makes a bohemian gown edgy with a tough black heel and feather headdress.

Here, a '70s-style fur is worn with a print top and floppy hat.

To tweak this sexy, curve-hugging minidress, Wasson adds a tomboy touch with booties.

EL AMOR NO HA MUERTO

'Art is the
guarantee
sanity'
Louis

9. People compliment my:
ability to make things look uncomplicated

19. Never: Stress fashion
It's fleeting. you miss a trend one
season, there's always a new one
around the corner

FALLING
IN LOVE
ROCKS

HER FAVORITE SHOPS

SURFING COWBOYS
*1624 Abbot Kinney
Boulevard
Venice, CA 90291*
(310) 450-4891

GYPSY T-SHIRTS
gypsy05.com

ALEXANDER WANG
shop.alexanderwang.com

20. Always: Wear jewlery the can double
as a weapon !! Never know when
it can come in handy

*The inspiration wall
in Wasson's apartment*

Wasson pairs her Alexander McQueen vest with jean shorts and red-carpet dresses alike.

A sexy black Alexander Wang dress is instantly punk when worn with studded biker boots.

Wasson's own cross design for Low Luv

Wasson's regular uniform revolves around a slouchy white T-shirt like this one by Kain.

Tough-luxe accessories—like this Gucci bag and See By Chloé boots—add the perfect counter-balance to cutoffs.

WASSON PUTS HER ALTERNATIVE DOWNTOWN SPIN ON VINTAGE FINDS AND AMERICAN CLASSICS.

As the widely recognized godmother of the ever-popular MOD (model-off-duty) look, Wasson has an expertly disheveled style that is a seamless blend of her past and present. Bringing her Texan tendencies (cutoffs and Hanes T-shirts) to her life as a model and designer in Manhattan (McQueen jackets and Alexander Wang rock-star dresses), Wasson prefers a look that can go from day to night with a minimum of feminine fuss. For example, pairing a slouchy men's silk shirt with her signature Daisy Dukes, plus a tangle of sexy chain necklaces from her line, Low Luv, will take the model from strolling the East Village to a Fashion Week afterparty. The rebellious beauty's only rule? Keep your clothing basic, and then "add your flair" with personal jewelry.

"I GREW UP IN TEXAS, A DENIM-OBSESSED STATE. I'D GO TO THE THRIFT STORE AND FIND LEVI'S 501s, AND THE NATURAL THING WAS TO JUST CUT THEM OFF."

— ERIN

Pair these sexy shorts with a simple white T-shirt and add personality with layers of long, sexy chain necklaces or a handful of silver and turquoise rings, as Wasson does.

LAKSHMI, PHOTOGRAPHED AT HOME IN THE EAST VILLAGE.

Opposite from left: Lakshmi's antique Maharani gold, uncut-diamond-and-emerald earrings; at two years old

Padma

PADMA LAKSHMI

URBAN SENSUALIST

OCCUPATION	*Model, cookbook author, jewelry designer, and host of Bravo's* Top Chef
BEST KNOWN FOR	*Bringing sophisticated sex appeal to reality TV*
HOME BASE	*East Village, New York City*

F OR PADMA LAKSHMI, fashion sometimes inspires lunch—or vice versa. "Maybe I'll open my dressing-table drawer and see an armlet I bought one day in Marrakesh, and I'll remember stopping for lunch in the middle of the souk that day, having this beautiful tagine, preserved lemons smothered all over steaming baked chicken," she says. "What can I do to evoke that taste, the dark romance of that faraway land?"

So she throws preserved Moroccan lemons (one of those things she just happens to have on hand) into a blender along with a spoonful of honey, a couple of red chilies, a knob of ginger. This she spreads on crusty bread for a meal that is about flavors but also accessories, nostalgia, and adventure—Padma's world, on toast.

Lakshmi's ruby-and-diamond handpiece; *below:* In full regalia at her 2004 wedding to Salman Rushdie; *opposite:* Wearing a beaded stole

It's no surprise that listening to Lakshmi talk makes your mouth water. Even when she's not eight months pregnant, there's something luscious about this woman. (It's the reason we love to watch her eat—not nibble—her way through the contestants on Bravo's beloved cooking show, *Top Chef.*) And just a few weeks before the birth of her daughter, Krishna, Lakshmi is draped across an antique divan, her body swathed in creamy folds of Lanvin, her feet and ankles encircled in delicate gold chains, looking positively fecund—a fertility goddess in repose in her East Village apartment. When she claims that pregnancy has been "glorious, joyous, fun, sexy," you can't help but believe her.

Still, for all her lush femininity, Lakshmi is also unmistakably determined. Only a few years ago, her claim to fame was tenuous. She was recognizable to fashion lovers as a successful ex-model and had hosted an Italian TV show, but was best known in America as Salman Rushdie's wife. Today, three years after their divorce, she has a cookbook, *Tangy Tart Hot & Sweet;* a gig on Emmy-nominated *Top Chef;* and her own jewelry line (which is helmed in the chic atelier-slash-test-kitchen on the top floor of her apartment building).

Lakshmi came by her strong will naturally: She was raised by a single mother who left India for New York City to escape the stigma of divorce in her home country. Evidence of her tough streak is written, quite literally, on her arm; for our photo shoot, she speci-

THE ELLEMENTS OF PADMA

"I didn't really wear pregnancy clothes; I just worked with what was already in my closet," says Lakshmi, wearing a gathered Lanvin dress and a dramatic Chanel collar of gold feathers.

fied that the seven-inch scar left by a car accident when she was 14 was not to be retouched. In fact, that scar has become something of a style signature for her—she never shies from displaying it on her show and the red carpet.

A modern gypsy, Lakshmi uses her treasures to track her journeys, both literal and spiritual. "I've traveled all over the world, so I feel as much Italian and Mediterranean as I do Indian, and I certainly feel like an American girl, because I grew up here," she says. "But my attitude toward jewelry is incredibly Indian. We commemorate everything with jewelry and food."

For years, she celebrated every milestone with the purchase of a new piece of jewelry. And so, besides the rustic wooden swing that hangs smack in the middle of her living room—how's that for sexy?—the multihued stacks of Indian shawls and saris, the antique military jackets, the glittering "eveningwear closet," and the shelf full of Hermès bags (some still unused), the main attraction in her home is the baubles.

Her jewelry is draped around dress forms, hung from mirrors, and crowded into a multitier glass armoire. But the real treasures reside in what she calls the "jewelry archive"—a Wild West–style safe

that takes up one corner of her bedroom. At Lakshmi's command, an assistant extracts tray after tray from its belly: Fred Leighton diamond earrings; a Verdura charm bracelet; a chunky rose-gold Rolex; a 1920s Vacheron Constantin watch; piles of antique, rich yellow Mughal jewelry; and a yards-long string of diamonds. Of a long, beaded necklace gifted to her by a Masai tribesman, during a trip to Africa, she quips, "I think I may have promised to marry him and skipped town. Not the first time I've done that for a necklace!"

Lakshmi's jewelry doesn't just lie in state. She puts it to good use, repurposing antique necklaces as belts and dressing up sexy draped jersey dresses with stacks of antique bangles and chandelier earrings from India. ("People swear you can only wear a dress once on the red carpet, but I wear the same ones again and again," she says. "If you change the accessories, no one can tell.") But she also buys with the seriousness of a collector—one who frequently falls for not-so-practical *objets*. Certain pieces, she admits, rarely come out of the safe. But so what? "They'll be one instrument that you may hear only every seven minutes in a big opus," she says. "But won't that opus be more beautiful with this little piccolo in it?"

"MY ATTITUDE TOWARD JEWELRY IS INCREDIBLY INDIAN. WE COMMEMORATE EVERYTHING WITH JEWELRY AND FOOD."

PADMA

Lakshmi's Indian roots are part of her style.
From left: Padma's uncle Ravi, mom, uncle Vichu, grandfather, and grandmother

Above: Lakshmi as the face of "The New India" in 2006; *top right:* The same antique sari she wore on the *Newsweek* cover

PADMA'S WORLD

Treasures are amassed (and artfully displayed) for easy access in Lakshmi's house. Here, necklaces are draped across a mirror. *Below:* A collection of bangles adorns a sculpture in her dressing room.

Many items from Lakshmi's own jewelry line—seen here in the atelier above her apartment—are inspired by the vintage pieces she's been collecting all her life.

Antique white jade, ruby, emerald, and diamond earrings

A Francesco Clemente portrait, a joint gift from Rushdie and the artist, hangs over her bed. *Below:* For guests, Lakshmi serves exotic spiced teas infused with flower petals.

Lakshmi's bedroom safe functions as top security for her jewels as well as a bedside table.

Swoon-worthy Roger Vivier heels in a print "inspired by Monet's paintings of Giverny"

INSPIRATION BOARD

For Padma, it's all
intertwined: "Spices,
teas, jewelry, beautiful
dresses, lovely fabrics. It's
all style," she says.

4. The most reliable thing in my closet: My old RAF military
jacket bought years ago at Portobello Market -
my old neighborhood in Notting Hill, London.
It looks great with jeans, leather pants,
or even a cocktail dress. Plus I love the
history of it.

Left: An abstract Ganesh gold
pendant draped over a framed
picture of Lakshmi's aunt Neela;
right: Lakshmi with her cousin
Rajni and nephew Sidhanth

2. <u>Dorothy Parker</u> is my style icon because: of her sharp wit and literary panache. Whatever she actually dressed like, her style of being, living and commicating show enduring iconic status through the decades.

Lakshmi's niece Iva in a carved, antique silver frame

Lakshmi's beauty icon: Bollywood actress Sharmila Tagore, seen here in '70s classic Amar Prem—her "eye makeup and saris are so beautiful," says Lakshmi.

Lakshmi, at seven years old, in a photo taken at her grandfather's sixtieth birthday in South India

PADMA MAKES HER PERFUME AT HOME, TAILORING HER SCENT TO HER MOOD. HERE, ONE OF HER FAVORITE RECIPES.

25 DROPS NEROLI ESSENTIAL OIL
30 DROPS GERANIUM ESSENTIAL OIL
20 DROPS ROSE ESSENTIAL OIL

10 DROPS MANDARIN OR TANGERINE ESSENTIAL OIL
5 DROPS BAY OR LAUREL-LEAF ESSENTIAL OIL
JOJOBA OIL FOR BODY, BATH, OR MASSAGE OIL

FOR CONCENTRATED PERFUME:
"Mix the above into 1/2 ounce of jojoba oil, then pour it into a vial with a tight lid through a small funnel. After bathing, dab on pulse points and rub a few drops into the ends of long hair in the summer."

FOR BODY, BATH, OR MASSAGE OIL:
"Mix the above quantities of essential oils into 4 ounces of jojoba oil and shake vigorously before each use."

3. The sexiest thing in my closet: A great pair of Armani Four jeans that are pencil thin and really sexy. Very Mick Jagger. They're old and faded and make me feel spiderlike. They look great with a T-shirt, a crisp man's shirt or even sequins and strappy heels.

FASHION AND ACCESSORIES

This namesake "Padma" dress by Costello Tagliapietra pairs loose draping (a Lakshmi signature) with a figure-flattering defined waist. Dress it down for day with ethnic-inspired wood-and-silver jewelry, or make it stand out for night with bold chandelier earrings.

Lakshmi loves menswear tailoring, especially her collection of vintage English and Russian military jackets. This Chris Benz jacket lightens up the look.

Wear your adventures on your arm, as Lakshmi does. Casual, hand-hewn accessories, like this bangle by M.C.L, reflect a melting pot of cultures.

Perfect for strolling far-flung bazaars or city streets, these Brian Atwood flat metallic sandals add a hint of easy exoticism.

Beading dresses up a Dries Van Noten evening bag.

LAKSHMI'S APPETITE FOR HISTORY, ART, AND CULTURE IS WOVEN INTO HER WARDROBE.

Lakshmi has created outfits inspired by Degas ballerinas and a painting of a gypsy at the Metropolitan Museum of Art; on the red carpet, she's as likely to wear a necklace given to her by an African tribesman as a glittering strand of Fred Leighton diamonds. Her favorite things bear the softness and patina of time: precious antique saris, hand-woven shawls, vintage jewelry from every conceivable era. But she always mixes the old with the new, choosing bold colors as rich as those in her well-stocked spice cabinet: saffron, mustard, aubergine, and jade. And accessories, of course, are her strong suit. Even if she's wearing jeans and an American Apparel tank top, she tops it off with "gorgeous, drop-dead jewelry."

"THE MOST MONEY I'VE EVER SPENT WAS ON AN ACCESSORY, NEVER A DRESS."

PADMA

Lakshmi adores opulent jewels, like this oversize necklace by Iradj. You don't have to be a Mughal princess to get the look: Street fairs, markets, and antique stores can yield precious-looking finds at mere-mortal prices.

FERGIE, PHOTOGRAPHED
IN A DOLCE & GABBANA
BODICE IN NEW YORK CITY'S
THOMPSON HOTEL.

Opposite: A sketch of a spikes-and-
chain-mail minidress by The Blonds for
the Black Eyed Peas' 2010 The E.N.D.
tour—and the real thing

FERGIE

ROCK-STAR FABULOUS

OCCUPATION	*Singer, Black Eyed Peas frontwoman*
BEST KNOWN FOR	*Propelling Fergaliciousness to the top of the charts*
HOME BASE	*Brentwood, Los Angeles*

ERGIE MAY BE FAMOUS for her "lady lumps," but in person, she's a slip of a thing who looks even tinier amid her seemingly constant swarm of handlers and admirers. Other celebrities may hunker down behind their glasses and bodyguards, but Fergie navigates this melee with an outsize, generous charm—she has the disarming habit of grabbing the hand or forearm of whomever she's talking with, creating intimacy in the midst of chaos. So when she walks into a photo shoot at the bar of SoHo's Thompson Hotel, hugging publicists and smooching hairstylists, it's all smiles...and one collective question mark: *This* is Fergalicious? Her three-quarter-length black jacket is beautifully cut and elegant, but verging on monastic—not what you expect from a woman known for her, er, bare necessities.

Not to worry. Within seconds, she has shed the coat to reveal a corseted floral-print Dolce & Gabbana—romper? Onesie? Bathing costume? Whatever you call it, it's just the sort of utterly impractical yet fabulous garment one hopes famous pop stars with hot movie-star husbands (in her case, Josh Duhamel) have on hand, if only for swanning around the perimeter of their swimming pool.

Twenty minutes later, the photographer has his shot, and Fergie—in yet another completely different incarnation perhaps best described as Janis Joplin gone pop: fluffy faux fur, leather leggings, and ginormous round sunglasses—is hopping into an ominous-looking black van. She's bound for Madison Square Garden, where she will do a handful of radio interviews before taking the stage in front of 14,000 screaming fans—a full house—with her fellow Black Eyed Peas. This is what Fergie's life is like these days. The pace seems impossible, but for a girl who's been plotting her success since age eight, it ain't half bad.

"There's something that turns on in me when I walk out onto that stage," she says. "I see the people, and the music starts, and no matter how tired I am, something just naturally happens, and I'm in it." Performing, after all, is the part she dreamed of as a kid in La Habra, California, when she was mimicking Andrea McArdle's Annie and, later, doing pitch-

perfect renditions of Donna Summer and Laura Branigan. Midway through tonight's concert, she will tear up believably when it's time for her solo "Big Girls Don't Cry" (one of three number-one hits from her 2006 solo album, *The Dutchess*). "Playing Madison Square Garden!" she gasps, looking out at a sea of entranced fans. "It's a dream come true."

The sleek, grown-up jacket; the pinup romper; the rock-star layers—three totally different looks in less than an hour is nothing unusual for Fergie. Ask her about her uniform and she laughs: "There's no such thing." Her wardrobe, she says, is like her musical tastes: unpredictable. Her sound is pop, hip-hop, club-synthesized, with a little rap thrown in, plus a recent injection of gritty rock 'n' roll, and each of these genres has made its mark on her wardrobe.

Over the years, that has made for quite a style trajectory, one that evolved, she laughs, "in front of everybody." At age nine, after a string of

> **❝I LIKE NOT HAVING TO STICK TO ONE THING. JUST BECAUSE I'M DOING AN ELECTROPOP RECORD DOESN'T MEAN I'M NOT GOING TO PERFORM WITH SLASH.❞**
>
> FERGIE

Opposite: En route to Madison Square Garden in faux fur by Rachel Zoe and architectural Rick Owens boots

In 1984 a young Stacy Ferguson takes center stage on *Kids Incorporated.*

Backstage at Madison Square Garden with fellow Peas Taboo and Apl.de.ap— "We're all a bunch of misfits, but it works. We all just get along and let ourselves be free," she says.

commercials for things like Duncan Hines, Stacy Ferguson got her first big gig: as one of the bubbly preteens in layered socks and curly side ponytails on the weekend variety show *Kids Incorporated*, alongside Mario López, Jennifer Love Hewitt, and future late-'80s pop star Martika.

At 16, she switched gears dramatically, joining Wild Orchid, the girl group she would stick it out with for 10 years. Her look was extremely blond, toned, and tan, with a fondness for shiny outfits coordinated to match her bandmates'. In 2002, recast as "Fergie," she joined the Peas, then an indie-leaning rap outfit. Her wardrobe was both sexed-up and willfully sporty, as if to prove she was one of the guys, not a mere hood ornament. "I'd throw on Dickies and a wife-beater and call it a day," she says. "I was such a tomboy in that phase of my life. Becoming comfortable being completely feminine was a process." Still, she wasn't shy about making her body a focal point: The Dickies were

often accompanied by tank tops slashed to reveal washboard abs, and the tank top was often sequined, slashed, and paired with skirts that covered less than some belts do. It was a mix of girl-next-door and the girl who pops out of the cake, and it got plenty of attention.

With *The Dutchess*, Fergie was determined "to represent me, separate from the Black Eyed Peas," she says. "The album was all about tying everything that inspires me into one: Skater meets old-school hip-hop meets a sort of B-girl meets a little bit of L.A. chola style." It was her idea to riff on a British theme with her "naughty, naughty" single "London Bridge" and a look that, if not exactly a hit with fashion critics, did make its point: bowler hats, microscopic Burberry-print shorts, white blouses knotted at the midriff.

These days, Fergie seems to be experiencing something of a fashion breakthrough, both personally and professionally. The Peas' record-

breaking album *The E.N.D.* proclaimed the band ahead of the pack: "I'm so 3008; you're so 2000 and late," she says in "Boom Boom Pow." The vibe, she says, was "sci-fi, superhero, futuristic, Mad Max," and it merited an image overhaul. At her urging, the Peas "decided to really up our game in the show department," she says. They invested in a mammoth, largely chrome-plated wardrobe, overseen by insider-beloved stylist and costume designer B. Akerlund, including custom pieces commissioned from L.A.'s punk-rock-meets-fashion duo The Blonds. "One of my costumes was made in Japan," says Fergie. "While I'm performing, it opens up, almost like a birth, and reveals this huge, lit-up orchid." Fergie alone has six costume changes per night. "It's crazy backstage," she says. "It's chaotic, frenetic, and then you just kind of take a breath and you get back out there." Offstage, her wardrobe has been headed in a totally different direction, inspired in part by an unlikely friend-

Tour wardrobe director Chris Psaila makes a last-minute adjustment to a Geiger-inspired suit by designer Michael Schmidt. *Right:* Onstage in front of a sold-out crowd

Lounging in a Céline jacket and a Dolce & Gabbana dress

"THERE IS NO UNIFORM: IT DEPENDS ON IF I'M FEELING A LITTLE MORE ROCK 'N' ROLL, OR BOHEMIAN, OR CASUAL."

— FERGIE

ing out "Sweet Child o' Mine" with Slash the next. "On some days I love to chill, and the more bohemian side comes into play," she says. On others, she shows up smart and sexy on Duhamel's arm—something she's been doing with new confidence of late. Being both diminutive and busty, she does not have the easiest shape to dress. A frock that would appear demure on someone less well-endowed can look obvious on her; plunging necklines, ruffles—it doesn't take much to go over the top. But in recent years, Fergie has been meeting designers and enjoying a front-row seat where fashion happens. "I've been finding the more elegant side of fashion, becoming comfortable with that," she says. On the red carpet, she's discovered what works: sweeping goddess gowns and curve-hugging, clean-lined minidresses.

Of course, when you have multiple fashion personalities, you need a place to store them all. Luckily, Fergie has "a good husband who knows I'm a pack rat." When they moved into their Brentwood, California, manse, she and Duhamel knocked down the wall between two guest rooms and turned the space into a "rock 'n' roll boudoir-themed closet with chandeliers and zebra-lined floors," she says. A third guest room became what she calls "my baby"—a room just for fittings, full of hats, bags, and scarves for easy styling. But her favorite part is the "treasure chest": a mirrored accessories cabinet so tall and so wide, with so many little drawers, that "it's like a store," she says. It even locks via remote control. *So* 3008.

ship with guitar god Slash. The two have been playing together on and off since 2008; Fergie was the only woman to sing on his self-titled album in 2010. "He started coming to play with me at a lot of my shows," she recalls. "We were doing this rock 'n' roll medley with a mixture of Rolling Stones and Led Zeppelin, Sublime, and 'Barracuda'. Little by little, this rock 'n' roll thing started to make its handprint on my wardrobe—leather pants, chrome crosses."

"I like not having to stick to one thing," she says. "Just because I'm doing an electro-pop based record doesn't mean I'm not going to perform with Slash." And just because she's stalking Madison Square Garden one day dressed as C-3PO's fantasy lady-bot doesn't mean she's not going to be slithering around in leather, screech-

Above, from left: *Fergie, circa 1985; a costume sketch by Michael Schmidt; the light-up "orchid" dress by Yuimana Kazato, shown open and closed; below: A costume sketch by Todd Lynn*

THE BEHIND-THE-SCENES SCOOP ON FERGIE'S TOUR WARDROBE

Fergie's futuristic wardrobe for The E.N.D. tour with the Black Eyed Peas was masterminded by costume designer B. Akerlund. "The entire show was in keeping with the '3008' theme from our album, *The E.N.D.*," says Fergie. "It's sci-fi fashion with a lot of chrome and metal."

15. When I fell in love I was wearing:

LOTZ of THINGS. U DONT FALL IN LOVE IN ONE DAY

10. I wish I could change my:

BIG MOUTH ! :)

HER FAVORITE SHOPS

WALTER STEIGER
waltersteiger.com
417 Park Avenue
New York, NY 10022
(212) 826-7171

ETRO
etro.com
461 North Rodeo Drive
Beverly Hills, CA 90210
(310) 248-2855

ANONAME JEANS
anoname.com

LISA KLINE
1435 S. Robertson Blvd.
Los Angeles, CA 90048
(310) 385-7113

STYLE STUDY

Fergie tucks in the edge of her slouchy T-shirt to maintain a figure-flattering shape.

Her classic updo and demure t-straps balance the sex appeal of a peekaboo neckline.

A studded belt, stacked bangles, and tough heels temper the sweetness of this femme dress.

FASHION AND ACCESSORIES

Skinny acid-wash Diesel Black Gold jeans get down and dirty with T-shirts or clean up nicely with a simple tailored jacket and heels.

A statement bag, megashades, and sky-high heels take a vintage rock tee to pop-star heights.

Petite, curvy girls like Fergie do best in shorter, body-conscious shapes like this Balmain minidress.

"I'll start with a bag," says Fergie, who will build a look around a splurge like this Christian Louboutin bag.

Fergie lives in ultrahigh heels; these, by Camilla Skovgaard, combine sporty traction with rock-star chain detail.

Fenton/Fallon spiked bangles are best by the armful.

WHETHER FERGIE IS ONSTAGE OR OFF, HER LOOK ALWAYS HAS AN ELEMENT OF PERFORMANCE.

Over nearly two decades in the spotlight, Fergie has test-driven countless looks. Today, she is a married woman with a solo album under her belt, so the personal style of the Black Eyed Peas' lone woman has reached new levels of sophistication. Equal parts heavy-metal cool—collaborating with former Guns N' Roses guitarist Slash allowed the "rock 'n' roll thing" to creep into her wardrobe—hip-hop fly girl, and fashion-forward temptress, Fergie's look is 100 percent rock star. Blackout sunglasses, corseted tops, punked-out heels, minishorts, and "rugged, distressed jeans"—they're all part of the singer's daring mix.

❝I THROW ON A PAIR OF SUNGLASSES AND I'M OUT THE DOOR.❞

FERGIE

No self-respecting rock goddess leaves home without her shades. Fergie switches between round, oversize frames and classic aviators—but when the goal is total fabulosity, Dolce & Gabbana rhinestone-studded wraparounds never hurt.

HUSTON, SHOT IN HER
VENICE BEACH HOME.
NECKLACE BY ARMANI.

Opposite: A photo from *Interview*
magazine; a portrait by
illustrator Mats Gustafsson

Angelica (signature)

ANJELICA HUSTON

ICONIC SIMPLICITY

OCCUPATION	_Actor, director_
BEST KNOWN FOR	_Roles in films as varied as_ Prizzi's Honor, The Addams Family, _and_ The Royal Tenenbaums
HOME BASE	_Venice, Los Angeles_

HE GIANT, BLOCKISH structure in the middle of Venice Beach, California, where Anjelica Huston lives is most often described as a fortress but is, in fact, a love nest. When the actress first started dating her husband, sculptor Robert Graham, she had a house in the hills of Benedict Canyon; he lived in the artists' enclave of Venice. "Courting" her, as she puts it, was an hour-and-a-half expedition each way. Still, Huston refused to move to Venice until their 1992 honeymoon in Oaxaca, Mexico, during which they stayed at a former monastery-turned-prison barracks that had been reimagined as the Presidente hotel. Within its high walls was an "incredibly welcoming" interior courtyard full of plants and flowers. "I thought, Well, if one were to build *this* way, I could live in Venice," she says. Graham asked her what she liked: high ceilings, curved walls, pyramid shapes, domes, and white. "So he built me my dream house," she says. A secret garden home that's "a little bit Bauhaus, a little bit Moorish, a little bit Spanish, a lot Mexican, and a little deco."

Two years after Graham's death after a short illness, living with—or rather *in*—this constant reminder "is unbearably sad on one level," Huston says, but also comforting. "I see him in every line. I see traces of him everywhere." Huston's home isn't just full of reminders of her marriage; it's chockablock with memorabilia from every phase of her life. "I'm what's known as a pack

rat," she says with a laugh. Not only does she save her costumes—*The Royal Tenenbaums'* "slightly below-the-knee, too-small suits" and signature locket are hidden away in a trunk somewhere, as is Morticia Addams' witchy black dress—she is also a hoarder of ephemera and oddities. "I'm one of those people who fill up counters and tabletops," she says. "I have *things*—photographs, objects, sculptures, Buddhas, crucifixes, octopi, Indian papier-mâché musicians...I have a relentless supply of items."

Like this place, Huston cuts an imposing figure but possesses a profound inner softness. She was born with a regal bearing; her royalty, of course, of the Hollywood variety. Her grandfather, Walter Huston, won an Oscar for his role in *The Treasure of the Sierra Madre,* a film that was directed by his son, Anjelica's father, the iconic John Huston, also the auteur behind *The Maltese Falcon* and *The African Queen.* When she was 18, John's daughter wasn't ready to take on that third-generation mantle; instead, in 1969, she moved to New York City, where legendary editor Diana Vreeland promptly dispatched her to Ireland for a fashion shoot with Richard Avedon. Long and lean, strong, and slightly androgynous, she possessed the elongated face and almond eyes of a Modigliani painting. Posing for David Bailey, Helmut Newton, and her longtime boyfriend, photographer Bob Richardson, Huston made fashion images that looked like art. In them, she is provocative, haughty, commanding, always with those long, sooty eye-

Above: Huston in a 1950s Balenciaga wrap from her mother, the ballerina Enrica "Ricky" Soma

66MY HUSBAND BUILT ME MY DREAM HOUSE: A LITTLE BIT BAUHAUS, A LITTLE BIT MOORISH, A LITTLE BIT SPANISH, A LOT MEXICAN, AND A LITTLE DECO.**99**

ANJELICA

lashes. But her look, she maintains, has always been a matter of genetics, not disposition. In her youth, Huston was convinced she looked horrible in pictures, that people only wanted to shoot her "because I was a famous man's daughter," she says. "I think women who are tall and dark with big shoulders *look* pretty commanding. In life, I'm not as strong as in my pictures. I'm a survivor, but I don't go down without a whimper, I'll say that. I'm a big crier. I'm a legendary weeper."

Still, that impressive physicality—combined with a unique voice that seems to ooze kindness, a voice made for storytelling—has defined a career with powerful high notes. She chooses brave, unpredictable roles: a con artist in *The Grifters*; a Holocaust survivor and wronged wife in *Enemies, A Love Story*; and in her Oscar-winning turn as Maerose, the daughter of a Mafia don in the black comedy *Prizzi's Honor* (co-starring Huston's longtime on-again, off-again love, Jack Nicholson, and directed by her father). And she slyly plays up her serious looks in quirky, offbeat projects, like the string of kooky mothers she's played in Wes Anderson's highly mannered movies *The Royal Tenenbaums, The Life Aquatic with Steve Zissou,* and *The Darjeeling Limited.*

As for Huston's iconic style, its foundation was laid when she was stalking the '70s runways of Giorgio Sant'Angelo and her friend Halston (and mingling with them at Studio 54, Elaine's, and Max's Kansas City). "Halston was incredibly sleek and polished and understated—very luxurious fabrics," says Huston, whose cool, leggy beauty made her the archetypal Halston woman. Still, she spent most of her time in blue jeans and crisp white shirts, old standards that remain her mainstays. "I always revert to that," she says. "Cowboy boots, jeans, white shirt. That will carry you across many borders."

Seventies style was luxe but, at its heart, was all about fluid simplicity, a tenet that Huston has stuck with. "I've found myself pretty much in black and white since then," she says. Simplicity complements her particular beauty but also serves a practical purpose: "Black-and-white is a good background for embellishment." Her flourishes come in the form of a lifetime's collection of jewelry: multicolored pearls (her birthstone), hammered gold-and-stone pieces from her friend, the jeweler Darlene de Sedle. "She made a beautiful ring that I love to wear, which is a big moonstone scarab set in gold," she says. "It makes me feel like a goddess."

> **❝I ALWAYS LIKED ACTING BECAUSE IT ALLOWS ONE TO CHOOSE TO BE STRONG. IN LIFE, I'M NOT AS STRONG AS IN MY PICTURES.❞**
>
> ANJELICA

Right: Huston photographed in April 1971; *opposite:* Strong monochromatic looks, like this Pamela Barish dress, provide the perfect backdrop for treasures from her jewelry box—in this case, a Cartier brooch that was a gift from her husband.

In a MaxMara gown and pearl earrings; *right:* An Italian wooden Adonis draped in Moroccan necklaces, brought back by her father after shooting *The Man Who Would Be King*

Amid the tchotchkes, her best supporting actress Oscar for *Prizzi's Honor* nestles next to a Golden Globe for *Iron-Jawed Angels*.

Her signature scent, Jean Patou's "1000"; *below:* A jewelry box circled with cameos holds her antique silver collection.

This eighteenth-century mirror—found by Huston and her mother during an antiquing trip—once hung in her childhood bedroom.

INSPIRATION BOARD

Clockwise from top left: with Jack Nicholson in the early '70s; a photograph from 1968; a sketch from The Addams Family

WITH AN EYE FOR PRECISION, HUSTON PREFERS A MONOCHROME CANVAS WITH A SPLASH OF EXUBERANT JEWELS.

Much like the clean aesthetic of one of her favorite designers, '70s legend Halston, Huston practices the art of streamlined elegance. She emphasizes her dramatic features with a look that seems forever fresh—pin-straight bob, sooty eyeliner—and as eternally cool in her fifties as it was in her twenties. As for clothes, she prefers a relatively clean slate that enables her to showcase "a bit of gold and a few diamonds" or bold-colored stones. Huston's love for details is shared by auteur Wes Anderson, who's cast her in three of his six films. "Wes is decisive, refined, and very cool. He has a very sharp eye," says Huston. "I like the way he sees things."

HER FAVORITE SHOPS

SUMIKO
3007 Main Street
Santa Monica, CA
90405
(310) 399-2803

ABC CARPET & HOME
888 Broadway
New York, NY 10003
(212) 473-3000

GIORGIO ARMANI
436 North Rodeo Drive
Beverly Hills, CA 90210
(310) 271-5555

MICHAEL KORS
360 North Rodeo Drive
Beverly Hills, CA 90210
(310) 777-8862

A drawing of the cast of The Addams Family, by Al Hirschfeld

4. The most reliable thing in my closet: Jeans and a white shirt and cowboy boots.

9. People compliment my: family. for all the right reasons—!

15. When I fell in love I was wearing: a silk dress from Hawaii, black and white and very breezy!

3. The sexiest thing in my closet: A black Burberry Alan's tuxedo and some naughty and beautiful Agent Provocateur lingerie that my friend Jerry Hall gave to me.

A fashion illustration of Huston in Prizzi's Honor, by famed costumer Donfeld

"I LOVE PEARLS. THEY'RE MY BIRTHSTONE, SO I HAVE A PARTICULAR FONDNESS FOR THEM."

ANJELICA

Huston wears pearls her own way, with the boldness of an artist (no sweet, ladylike strands for her!). Let a crisp white shirt serve as a neutral backdrop for showcasing a piece of Yael Sonia statement jewelry.

GREENE, PHOTOGRAPHED
OUTSIDE HER NORTH
HOLLYWOOD HOME WEARING
A PRABAL GURUNG GOWN.

Opposite: Marlo, her toy fox terrier

Ashley Greene (signature)

ASHLEY GREENE

SMART SEX APPEAL

OCCUPATION	*Actress*
BEST KNOWN FOR	*The role of Alice Cullen in* Twilight
HOME BASE	*North Hollywood, Los Angeles*

NOT LONG AGO, Ashley Greene was an unknown actress who paid the bills by hostessing at the Belmont, a Los Angeles restaurant. She didn't know much about Stephenie Meyer's monstrously successful tween vampire novel, *Twilight*, when she got the call that they were casting the film—this was *big*, her agent said. She auditioned five times, first for the lead role of Bella, then for Alice (the gorgeous pixie sister of dreamy lead bloodsucker Edward), and "was on pins and needles for months" until another call: She got it. Two weeks later, as she was heading off to Portland, Oregon, to begin filming, it dawned on her. "In that moment, I just knew my life was going to change," she says.

Little did she know. *Twilight* being the unique phenomenon that it is—

Greene raids her closet.

with a built-in, ravenous fan base— the roller coaster kicked off right away, with "Twihards" trekking into the woods in hopes of spotting the long-awaited film in the making. These days, strangers profess their love for her on a daily basis. One woman asked the 23-year-old to marry her own husband. "I was like, 'Are you trying to pawn him off on me, or is this some open marriage?'" says Greene. "She was serious!"

In her hometown of Jacksonville, Florida, Greene was an all-star cheerleader in a no-joke league: four-hour daily practices, meets televised on ESPN. (Twihards, she notes with some surprise, have yet to dig up team photos of her, despite the "really small" uniform: a blue-green and white supershort skirt with side slits and a sports-bra top.) She attended a magnet high school with a focus on law, but at a certain point realized she was more interested in *acting* like a lawyer than in being one. She spent the next year using her courtroom coaching to cajole her parents into letting her move to L.A. "I know what I want when I want it, and there's no exception," she says. "I'm a very driven person." By 17, she had made the move.

"I am, at this moment, a kid in a candy shop," she says. In short order, she has shot two more *Twilight* installments—*New Moon* and *Eclipse*—plus the psychological thriller *The Apparition*, and an ensemble comedy, *Butter*.

In Hollywood, when you have the face of a pixie and the body of, well, an ESPN cheerleader, there will always be pressure to go in an obvious sartorial direction. "In the beginning, I was listening to stylists. They all want to make you look sexy, and they want you to wear the next big thing," she says. "Honestly, for me, if you're always wearing the next big

thing, then you don't have a sense of personal style." Now she has a rule: "You can't let other people dress you. They can bring you clothes, but you need to be the one who's picking what to wear."

Now that she's in charge, it's all about clean-lined shapes by designers who have sex appeal down pat: Dolce & Gabbana, Antonio Berardi, and relative newcomer Prabal Gurung. For premieres, floor-length, straight dresses that drop alluringly off one shoulder leave much to the imagination. "You can see your figure—it's form-fitting, it's sexy, but it doesn't have to be overtly sexy," she says. She also believes in "certain staples": a button-down white shirt, a pair of "really amazing" jeans (hers are by J Brand), a great pair of black heels, and a serious bag...or four. On a recent trip home from London, Greene made a point to get to the airport two hours early for a duty-free spree that yielded a quartet of arm candy: two Guccis, a Marc Jacobs, and a Burberry. "I knew that I was going to have them forever," she says apologetically. And with blockbuster bucks to spend and scripts piling up at her door, why resist?

As Alice Cullen, pixie vampire, in *New Moon; opposite:* In a ruffled confection by Ina Soltani

> **"I'VE ALWAYS BEEN THAT TYPE OF PERSON—I KNOW WHAT I WANT WHEN I WANT IT."**
>
> —— ASHLEY

INSPIRATION BOARD

A still from Twilight; Greene's bedroom door, decorated with memorabilia

2. **Audrey Hepburn** is my style icon because: She represents beauty, grace and class. She was timeless. Audrey's style came from who she was & what she represented — not just the clothes on her back

FOR GREENE, LOOKING STUNNING IS ALL ABOUT FOCUSING ON SIMPLE, EYE-CATCHING PIECES.

With just two years of *Twilight* fame under her belt, Greene has managed to dodge the fashion bullets that hit most red carpet newcomers. Eschewing overbearing stylists and It designers in favor of clean column dresses that are "sleek but not overdone," simple tailored jackets, and investment accessories, the former cheerleader lets her delicate features—and killer body—take center stage. Understanding the difference between "sexy and skanky" is a must, says Greene, who has found that looking beautiful is "all about balance."

STYLE STUDY

Tailored, figure-defining dresses are key to Greene's streamlined style.

Textured fabrics, booties and an oversize clutch add modernity to a classic shape.

For a high-necked LBD, Greene wisely keeps her hair pulled back and ultrasimple.

A still from New Moon

16. The **moment** that changed my life:
   1. I got on a plane to L.A.
   2. I booked Twilight

> **"I THINK A CLASSIC PAIR OF HEELS IS ESSENTIAL. IF YOU HAVE THE STAPLES, YOU CAN BUILD YOUR OUTFIT AROUND THEM."**

ASHLEY

Greene has an eye for reinvented classics. Take her lead and try a coy Maryjane, like this one by Christian Louboutin, instead of the standard ice-pick stiletto.

ROSS, PHOTOGRAPHED AT
HOME IN HER ART-LINED
STAIRWELL WEARING
'80S VINTAGE.

Opposite: Diana Ross's Maud Frizon
roller skates from the '70s

TRACEE ELLIS ROSS

MODERN ECLECTIC

OCCUPATION	*Actress*
BEST KNOWN FOR	*The role of Joan Clayton on* Girlfriends
HOME BASE	*Hollywood Hills, Los Angeles*

WITH HER enormous, almond-shaped eyes and cut-glass cheekbones, actress Tracee Ellis Ross doesn't need *that* last name to hint at her legendary lineage—it's written across her face. It's also evident from even a cursory glance into her closet. How many women, after all, are stocked up on rainbow-colored caftans, Maud Frizon roller skates, and enough sunglasses, boots, and bags to open a vintage store? Of Diana Ross's five children, Tracee was the one who really took to fashion, the one who hid backstage during concerts to help her mom slip from one spangled-and-feathered Bob Mackie confection to the next. "I would always be given some sort of assignment," she says. "Clipping on the earrings, or zipping her up, or helping her get her shoes on. I know how to butterfly a dress so she can step into it and continue changing her lipstick—which, of course, she did for every look."

In Ross's own career—including the role of Joan Clayton, the neurotic lawyer-turned-restaurateur she played for eight seasons on the sitcom *Girlfriends*—clothing has been "such a big part of how I find a character." She's currently developing a one-woman show populated with audacious, campy-yet-poignant caricatures, many of whom were born from her own closet. "Sabine," for instance, is a dating coach with "a lot of hair and boobs," says Ross in Sabine's breathy,

vampy voice. "She's got this huge, major push-up bra and something that shows off her decolalalala"—the word trails off ditzily—"and a pencil skirt with these crazy little cookie shoes." The character named "Fear," on the other hand, is an entirely different animal: a Southern madam whose prostitutes are the manifestations of anxiety. ("The agoraphobe is a great whore," Ross says drily. "She never leaves the house.") Fear wears an appropriately hideous getup: a velour sweatsuit with green stockings, "this crazy wig, and a pair of old Versace prescription glasses—I love them so much—they're horrid," Ross hoots.

Ross has more than enough gear to dress herself and an army of alter egos. Clothes and accessories stray from her

meticulously organized walk-in closet (where accessories are arranged boutique-style, rather than packed away, for easy perusal) into every room of her house, including the office, where a cabinet is stuffed with an anthology of Azzedine Alaïa she began collecting as a teenager.

In high school, Ross obsessed over Fiorucci and pilfered Alaïa, Norma Kamali, and Ghost from her mother's closet. "We had a big joke that when my mom would leave for work, she couldn't make it out of the driveway before I would go into her closet," she says. On Ross's eighteenth birthday, the mother-daughter duo flew to Paris on the Concorde to walk Thierry Mugler's runway. The footage—which Ross happily whips out—shows Tra-

" MY GUIDE FOR EVERYTHING: WHAT MAKES MY HEART SING? "

TRACEE

Above: On the antique iron bed that sits invitingly outdoors on her back patio, wearing a caftan "borrowed" from her mother; *opposite:* In fringed Christian Louboutin boots and Marc Jacobs shorts

> **❝I'VE BEEN DRESSING AUTHENTICALLY FOR ME—NOT FOR ANYBODY ELSE—FOR YEARS. SO IT'S NOT ABOUT WHAT'S GOING TO BE 'IN' BUT WHAT'S GOING TO WORK ON ME.❞**
>
> TRACEE

cee in a shiny black pleather suit and Diana in a Vegas-worthy glow-in-the-dark butterfly dress, cavorting, hand in hand, down the runway alongside Linda, Christy, and Naomi. ("My idols," says Ross.) By that age, the younger Ross was already becoming a known clothes hound; she remembers lecturing her less wardrobe-centric sister on the art of shopping: "It's a 24-hour-a-day, seven-day-a-week affair. You never know when you're going to get hit with something good."

These days, while "shopping trips at Mom's" are still a common occurrence, Ross's rate of consumption has mellowed considerably. "I'm not big on fashion," she says. "I'm big on *style.* I compare the difference to that between religion and spirituality." After years of trial and error, she's found a look that reflects who she is, one based on "strong lines, bold pieces, whimsy, sex appeal, elegance," she says. "Femininity, not girly-ness—I love woman." She knows what works: sheath dresses; clean-cut, high-waisted trousers (worn

with thin T-shirts); pencil skirts; and a foundation of vintage pieces from the late '70s and early '80s. Splurges from Balenciaga and Alexander McQueen are carefully considered. "I leave things on hold for a week or more," she says. "If I don't keep thinking about it, I don't need it."

Indeed, for a diva's daughter, Ross has some remarkably thrifty habits. "I do get rid of things but every time, I regret it," she says. A brown velvet blazer procured "for about $18.50 at the Salvation Army in college" was so perfect, she had it copied by a tailor twice. One of her couches has survived since college, too, in "at least four" incarnations, most recently a soft, silvery velvet.

For this unrepentant lover of things, clothes are self-expression but also evidence of personal history. "The way I dress is the way I decorate, the way I eat, the way I live," says Ross. "You could point to anything in my house and I could tell you where I found it, who gave it to me, what it means, and what the story is behind it."

Her "A-number-one" inspiration, mom Diana Ross, onstage in a sequined bathing suit in New York's Central Park, 1983

On her mother: "The person that people don't know is the mother that she is—the most generous, big-hearted person in the world with her children."

TRACEE'S WORLD

A Murano glass chandelier from an antique store in L.A.: "I had always dreamed of having jewelry on my ceiling!" *Left:* A framed image of Diana Ross

A view from the backyard

Right: "Just me being silly: I thought 'Tee Love' was a decent street name. I'd bought the fake LV bag and decided it was the perfect canvas for some legal graffiti."

Balenciaga shoes get pride of place in her wardrobe.

Ross's most prized possessions: Warhol sketches of her and of her sisters, which hang over a silver velvet couch

Ross's trusty companion, Lady Bug; right: '80s boots, a Diana Ross relic

HER FAVORITE SHOPS

DES KOHAN
*671 South Cloverdale
Avenue
Los Angeles, CA 90036
(323) 857-0200*

COQUETTE
*950 Hancock Avenue
West Hollywood, CA
90069
(310) 289-9199*

KAYO O'YOUNG
kayooyoung.com

DANIELA
*1003 North Fairfax
Avenue
West Hollywood, CA
90046
danielakurrlecouture.com*

LAWSON-FENNING EAST
*1618 Silverlake
Boulevard
Los Angeles 90026
(323) 660-1500
lawsonfenning.com*

Fledgling fashionista: Tracee, at right, does watercolors in shades.

2. **My MoM** is my style icon because:

she was, is and always will be Amazing!
... and I get all her clothes.

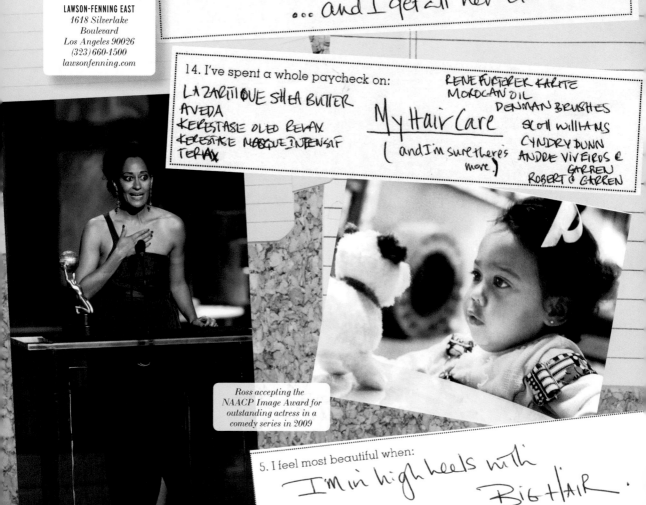

14. I've spent a whole paycheck on:

LA ZARTIQUE SHEA BUTTER
AVEDA
KERESTASE OLEO RELAX
KERESTASE MASQUE INTENSIF
TERAX

RENE FURTERER KARITE
MOROCAN OIL
DENMAN BRUSHES
SCOTT WILLIAMS
CYNDRY DUNN
ANDRE VIVEIROS &
GARREN
ROBERT & GARREN

My Hair Care
(and I'm sure there's more.)

Ross accepting the NAACP Image Award for outstanding actress in a comedy series in 2009

5. I feel most beautiful when:

I'm in high heels with BIG HAIR.

❝I POLAROID MY OUTFITS. I'LL TELL YOU WHY: WHEN YOU LOOK IN A MIRROR, YOU CAN SEE YOUR FEELINGS. WHEN YOU LOOK AT A PHOTO, YOU SEE HOW YOU REALLY LOOK.❞

TRACEE

Follow Ross's lead and keep a camera in your dressing room. A quick snap can tell you if you're in need of a wardrobe change or ready to roll!

HENDRICKS, PHOTOGRAPHED
AT HER WILSHIRE HOME.

Opposite: A few favorite pairs of shoes

Christina

CHRISTINA HENDRICKS

SILHOUETTE SAVVY

OCCUPATION	*Actress*
BEST KNOWN FOR	*The role of* Mad Men *bombshell Joan Harris (née Holloway)*
HOME BASE	*Wilshire, Los Angeles*

On her alter ego: "To wear clothes the way Joan does—body-conscious, form-fitting things that aren't inappropriate but are definitely to her benefit—it shows how self-aware she is." *Opposite:* A flower pin adds insouciance to a seriously curvy dress by one of Hendricks' favorite designers, L'Wren Scott.

VER SINCE OFFICE manager extraordinaire Joan Holloway sashayed into the *Mad Men* office in a jewel-tone sheath that was precision-cut to follow her every contour, every eye in the room—and in living rooms across America—has been locked on her. Expressions like "va-va-voom" were invented to describe women like Christina Hendricks, who plays Joan, but it's not just her body that holds our attention: Joan oozes condescension and a bossy sex appeal that makes every gesture magnetic. "Joan is the kind of person who knows that every second, at least one person is watching her," says Hendricks. "Every time she stands or moves, she's doing it for someone else."

When *Mad Men* first hit, Hendricks, 35, was as "confused and surprised" as any woman would be to find that her body had become a cultural talking point. Hendricks had worked for years as a model before landing in TV-land with roles on *ER* and *Kevin Hill.* In all that time, no one had seemed particularly fascinated with her form. "It really is my body type; it's my mom's body type; it's how I grew up; it's how I've looked in other TV shows," she says. But when Joan entered the picture, "it was the first thing people were talking to me about."

Right away, she was credited with having ushered in a new era of volup-tuousness. Once the sheer strangeness of that wore off, she saw the benefit of the attention. "So many women have said encouraging things to me, told me it's been inspiring to them, that I feel like it is something to celebrate," she says and laughs. "Honestly, for people to be nice about anything is so darn rare in this town." (When nay-sayers remark on her cleavage-showcasing dresses, she shrugs: "I've had people be like, 'I can't believe she's wearing that—it accentuates her breasts!' Look, they're not going any-where. They *can't* be hidden!")

What does her husband, actor Geoffrey Arend of *(500) Days of Sum-mer,* whom she married in 2009, think of the world's fixation on his wife's particular assets? "He's like, 'I've been telling you this for years,'" she says.

The real Hendricks lacks even a hint of Joan's officiousness, but there is something old-fashioned about her. She says things like "shoot" and "darn," and favors clothes that hark back to bombshells of yore. That, plus her milky complexion and sweet halo of Titian-red curls, makes it all the more difficult to picture her first real fashion statement, as a teenage goth. Hendricks' father was in the U.S. Forest Service; when she was growing up, the family moved from forest to forest, landing in Tennessee, Oregon, Georgia, Idaho. ("When I go back to Idaho and I smell the farms and the cows, everyone says, 'It smells!' and

Among her scents, Hendricks' favorite, L'Artisan Parfumeur Premier Figuier; *right:* A sign of stardom—her own bobblehead

I'm like, 'It's home to me!' It's so comforting. There's definitely a small-town girl in me.")

But a move to Virginia when she was in high school rubbed her the wrong way. "It sounds silly, but that was the big city to me," she says. She wanted to stand out from her *Heathers*-esque schoolmates, to prove, "I'm nothing like you; I'm not mean and harsh and judgmental, and I'm not cheering on when people get in fights"—and she did it with black nails, black clothes, black lipstick, baby-powder-white face, and a bob "that changed from black to fire-engine red to purple, depending on the month." With the money from her first job as a shampoo girl at a local salon, she bought a black leather motorcycle jacket and knee-high Dr. Martens.

Nowadays her look—and her life— are the polar opposite: "Feminine and girly," she says. "I love ruffles and flowers and all those things that you would never see Joan in." With her figure, though, a little bit of froufrou goes a long way. "The key for me is tailoring and showing my waistline. I used to fight that, because I just loved these billowy, silky, romantic things that just didn't fit my body type," she says. "Finally, it was like, 'Okay, let other girls wear those.' I've got to recognize what works for me." She's gleaned some useful tips from Joan. "I've learned about tailoring and about what's most flattering. I've definitely stolen ideas from her," she says. Now when she goes shopping and falls in love with something that's not quite right—and finding something that fits perfectly off the rack is rare—"instead of going, 'Oh, shoot, it doesn't fit,' I go, 'How can I make it fit?'" she says. "Once you have that knowledge, you just know how much easier it makes your life."

Hendricks, photographed in her lobby, steps out in a ruffled Oscar de la Renta dress and a cheeky beret.

INSPIRATION BOARD

Left: *"It sounds trite, but I love Marilyn, with all of that tailoring and those '40s, '50s, and '60s shapes—she just got it right."*

WHEN IT COMES TO DRESSING HER EXCEPTIONAL CURVES, HENDRICKS REINS IN HER GIRLISH INSTINCTS AND GOES FOR HIGH-IMPACT SIMPLICITY.

Although the actress admits her personal style is more romantic than that of her TV alter ego, they do share the same philosophy on curves: If you've got them, emphasize them. Instead of feeling discouraged when something doesn't fit perfectly, Hendricks makes it work: "If I find a dress I love that's not for someone with my bust size, I'll take it to a tailor and have them add a piece of lace in the neckline, and suddenly, it's a whole new dress!" The model-turned-actress's secret is to find—and then tweak—pieces that accentuate and sculpt her figure, not hide it or tart it up.

HER FAVORITE SHOPS

L'WREN SCOTT
net-a-porter.com

JOHN GALLIANO AT BERGDORF GOODMAN
bergdorfgoodman.com

PORTS 1961
*8483 Melrose Place
Los Angeles, CA 90069
(323) 951-9696*

RALPH LAUREN
*141 North Robertson
Boulevard
Los Angeles, CA 90048
(310) 274-0171*

EBAY
eBay.com

STYLE STUDY

A relatively covered-up gown looks fresh in fire-engine red; nude lips are a sexy contrast to her clothes and hair.

Hendricks updates a below-the-knee cocktail dress with a slim belt and leg-elongating gold pumps.

This ruffled gown in peachy-pink still works because of its defined waist and sweetheart neckline.

Hendricks' rustic chandelier from the New York City restaurant Il Buco—where she and Arend wed in 2009

1. My most prized possession: *is my Warren Muller Chandalier from Il Buco in NYC. My husband proposed under it!*

14. I've spent a whole paycheck on: *a motorcycle jacket. My first paycheck from my first job at a hair salon. I was 15.*

66THE KEY FOR ME IS TAILORING AND SHOWING MY WAISTLINE.99

CHRISTINA

Hendricks has learned that diaphanous layers—her secret passion—aren't the most flattering for women with her build. Instead, she gets her fix of feminine whimsy with svelte dresses, like this Zac Posen stunner, that showcase her shape.

VON FURSTENBERG, PHOTOGRAPHED ON THE ROOF OF HER MEATPACKING DISTRICT HEADQUARTERS—A BACKDROP INCLUDES THE EMPIRE STATE BUILDING.

Opposite: DVF's patron saint, Wonder Woman, keeps watch over her Manhattan office.

DVF

DIANE VON FURSTENBERG

RELAXED GLAMOUR

OCCUPATION	*Designer*
BEST KNOWN FOR	*Bringing easy glamour to working women worldwide*
HOME BASE	*Meatpacking District, New York City, and Litchfield County, Connecticut*

BORN TO A WEALTHY Belgian family and married twice to royalty—first to Swiss-born Prince Egon von Furstenberg, then to entertainment-world mogul Barry Diller—Diane von Furstenberg never technically needed to work. But her career in fashion "gave me my independence," she says. Launched like a juggernaut in 1972 with a sliver of printed rayon known as the wrap dress, that career also made her one of the most iconic working women of our time. The dress was—is—genius. It defined the waist; covered the thigh; allowed ease of movement; slipped on like a second skin; could be packed, wrinkle-free, in the smallest of carry-ons; and, like von Furstenberg herself, made nine-to-five seem pretty damned sexy—all values that the brand (and the woman) continues to embody. Today, sitting in her fuchsia-walled office beneath a pair of Warhols bearing her own image, DVF, now a 63-year-old grandmother (one who tweets, snorkels, and installed a Pilates Reformer 30 feet from her desk), is all legs, fluffed-up curls, and feline sensuality. In short, she's still got "it."

ELLE: Diane, what's your earliest fashion memory?

DVF: My aunt had a very elegant boutique in Paris. I used to go there and work in her shop, fold the sweaters and things like that. I didn't think it had an impact on me, but I guess to some degree it did—she was selling brands that were all about jersey, and I remember also beautiful printed sweaters. But the first fashion thing I ever owned was when I was 18 and my boyfriend gave me a Pucci shirt. I loved it.

ELLE: Is that what piqued your interest in design?

DVF: It wasn't that I wanted to be a fashion designer when I grew up. But I did know what kind of woman I wanted to become. And I became that woman, very much so.

ELLE: What kind is that?

DVF: Independent, on the go. Driving the bus.

ELLE: You moved to New York in 1971, newly married, pregnant, and carting a trunk full of samples of T-shirt dresses and shirtdresses you had sewn up in Belgium. Less than five years later, you'd made millions.

DVF: It happened very, very fast. At the age of 30, you're on the cover of *Newsweek*? You know, that's a big deal. I went to the White House for the first time the same week, and everybody knew who *I* was—but I was

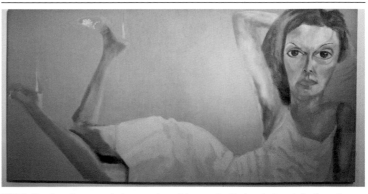

DVF in the dressing room in her apartment (conveniently located upstairs from her boutique and office); *above:* A Francesco Clemente portrait of the designer hangs in the lobby of her building.

On her desk, dozens of colored pens and pencils, poised should inspiration strike; among the works of art in her pink-walled office, *Untitled*, a life-size sculpture by John Battenberg

so impressed to be at the White House. You always see the woman across the room and you think, Oh my God, I'm so impressed to meet her, but that woman is impressed to meet you, you know?

ELLE: What's the essence of DVF style?

DVF: My clothes are all about within—what they do to you, to your psyche. What I like so much is to see different women wearing my clothes. One is pierced, in combat boots and blue hair; the other one has a string of pearls and lives on the Upper East Side. Madonna, for example, is a person who loves to shock, loves clothes and role play. But when Madonna wants to be herself—at the launch of her children's book, or for a meeting with the president of Argentina—strangely enough, she wears DVF.

ELLE: Showcase the woman; don't overpower her?

DVF: Exactly. It's the woman you should remember, not the dress, ever.

ELLE: Somehow, though, the DNA of your brand is always so closely—

DVF: —entwined with me? Not just with who I am but with what I believe in. It's about practicality and easiness. You know, the dresses are tools; they are friends. I always say that if this dress is not a friend, don't make it.

ELLE: How do you feel about aging?

DVF: I am one of those very few women who have decided not to do things to my face. Yes, I have facials, and I do this and that, but I don't inject anything. I feel like if I started to change myself, that would make me insecure. I'd rather be who I am and carry the memory

and the weight of what I've lived.

ELLE: You're so energetic! What keeps you going?

DVF: The two things that inspire me are nature and women. Nature because there you find everything—textures, prints, colors. I have a camera with me all the time. I hike and ski, and I also like the underwater, where it's endless in terms of beauty and colors. And then women...how they dress, what they wear, how they feel.

ELLE: Do you shop?

DVF: I don't buy any clothes. I splurged much more when I was young. Now I'm running out of space. But I will never stop buying books, twentieth-century furniture, textiles, jewelry—I have a big collection of Indian Mughal jewelry.

ELLE: And art, obviously? [Her office alone houses Warhols, Clementes, and countless other paintings and sculptures.]

DVF: I'm not a desperate collector. There's something about collecting that gives you anxiety. I just like what I like.

ELLE: So what do you spend on?

DVF: In this moment of my life, this third act, giving has become a big part of it. You pick up the phone or write one e-mail, and it will change somebody's life, and for you it was such a small effort. My mission in life is to empower women. I do it through fashion, through mentoring, through philanthropy. It's all one. When you get to my age, if everything around you—what you do and who you are and who your kids are and what you read, et cetera—if all of these things make sense and are coherent, then you have a successful life. That's it. That's your story.

"I FOUND MY VOICE. I FOUND MY STRENGTH. SO I'M VERY INSPIRED BY HELPING OTHER WOMEN FIND THEIRS."

DIANE

INSPIRATION BOARD

With Egon von Furstenberg in the early '70s

At then-husband Egon von Furstenberg's book party for The Power Look, *in New York City, 1978*

13. Every woman needs *herself !.*

3. The sexiest thing in my closet: *my fishnet stockings.*

10. I wish I could change my: *age !.! need more time.*

EVER SINCE HER STUDIO 54 DAYS, VON FURSTENBERG HAS WORKED THOSE GAMS!

When out on the town in the '70s, von Furstenberg never missed an opportunity to show off her stems with playful stockings. For your next big party, try a sheer black polka-dotted pair with a black microminidress.

With then-boyfriend (now husband) Barry Diller at Studio 54

DVF's priority has always been friends and family—as demonstrated by the crowded wall of her office. Right: In the '70s, soon after arriving in New York, she and then-husband Egon von Furstenberg were an It couple.

The consummate working woman in her workroom in 1973; below: Warhol portraits on the wall of her office

19. Never: lie

20. Always: love!

Above: *An iconic* Interview *cover; right: Steps from her desk, a Pilates Reformer for impromptu workouts*

FASHION AND ACCESSORIES

To capture DVF's breezy style, layer a printed dress with a relaxed trench, like this one from Gryphon. Push up the sleeves, pop the collar, and leave the jacket loose; the trick is the sense of ease.

A free-form Devi Kroell hobo in classic snakeskin is day-to-day functional yet sensual.

Thrown over a printed dress or casually tied, silky, oversize scarves add touchable luxe.

A classic pointy-toed Christian Louboutin pump (in leg-elongating nude) keeps a sack dress sexy.

DVF favors oversize jewelry in organic shapes—she designed this bracelet for H. Stern.

VON FURSTENBERG'S ENDURING SEX APPEAL IS ALL ABOUT RELAXED, WOMANLY LAYERS, RICH ACCESSORIES, AND A FRESH-FROM-VACATION VIBE, EVEN IN THE OFFICE.

Although von Furstenberg is one of the hardest-working women in fashion, nothing about her look reads business as usual. Her wardrobe evokes a sense of color, ease, and, most important, her joie de vivre. With her signature curls—which, even on the dreariest Manhattan day, look as if they've been wind-blown in the Mediterranean—von Furstenberg is perpetually zipped into one of her own colorful shifts. Whether it's a modern gold cocktail ring, an oversize semiprecious stone bracelet, or a spindly snakeskin sandal, von Furstenberg's finishing touches are always worldly and warm.

❝I CREATED A DRESS AND IT BECAME A SOCIAL PHENOMENON. THESE THINGS JUST HAPPEN.❞

DVF

Nothing says "DVF" like the designer's original wrap dress. Go for the full von Furstenberg effect and wear it with to-the-knee boots, nude fishnets, and a pair of gold hoops.

WILDE, PHOTOGRAPHED
AT HER VENICE HOME
IN A J.CREW DRESS.

Opposite: A preteen Wilde
on family vacation

Olivia

OLIVIA WILDE

BRAINY BOHEMIAN

OCCUPATION	*Actress*
BEST KNOWN FOR	*The role of sexy doctor Remy Hadley ("Thirteen") on TV megahit* House M.D.
HOME BASE	*Venice, Los Angeles*

THE ELLEMENTS OF OLIVIA

OLIVIA WILDE IS tough to typecast. She's a sylph, a sex symbol—and she once consumed 33 pancakes in 20 minutes to win an otherwise male-only Australian pancake-eating contest. She plays the drums and, as a teenager, dreamed of being a rapper. At 19, she wed filmmaker Tao Ruspoli, who happens to be descended from Italian royalty; they got engaged at Burning Man and said their vows in 2003 in a graffiti-covered, IKEA-outfitted school bus that was, at the time, their home. And she's surely the only woman to have topped the annual *Maxim* "Hot 100 List" who graduated from the cream of East Coast boarding schools (Phillips Academy), borrowed her stage name from Oscar Wilde, and was raised by a pair of award-winning journalists (Andrew and Leslie Cockburn) in Washington, D.C.'s intellectual swirl.

After high school, Wilde was bound for the theater program at Bard College in Annandale-on-Hudson, New York, when she abruptly changed course, moved to L.A., and quickly landed a role on the short-lived Jerry Bruckheimer series *Skin*, then a guest spot on *The OC*. In 2007 she joined Fox's medical mystery juggernaut, *House M.D.*, as bisexual smarty-pants doctor "Thirteen." Now she's gaining big-screen steam, setting the Comic-Con scene ablaze as cyberbabe Quorra in *Tron: Legacy*, the big-budget remake of the '80s sci-fi classic, and landing a starring role in the Jon Favreau–directed Wild West action blitz *Cowboys & Aliens.*

Wilde grew up a world away from blockbuster space invaders and babelicious photo shoots, in "a community that was focused on the important things happening throughout the world—politics and revolutions and life-or-death situations." As a child, she crawled under the dining-room table during dinner parties, sometimes falling asleep, but often "I just listened to the conversations, whether or not I understood them, enjoying the sound of everybody's voices and the debates," she says. "There was a sense of piqued interest at all times."

In this world, style wasn't regarded as frivolous—it was a form of empowerment. "That idea was instilled in me at a young age: that you can be an intelligent, powerful woman and also be a chic and beautiful and stylish woman. It wasn't like, 'Oh, that's silly. Don't think about those things.'" Whether she was reporting in Kabul or an African village, Wilde's mother was Hepburn-polished: white button-downs, cigarette pants, flats, and jewelry. "It was always about being graceful and elegant, and comfortable, too," Wilde says.

As a child, when Mom and Dad headed off to Taliban country, "I just thought of it in terms of what jewelry they'd bring back," she says, laughing. Afghanistan meant lapis and "amazing" embroidered jackets; Iraq, incredible hammered silver bangles. The gifts—still in heavy rotation in her wardrobe—taught her a lesson: "The Middle Eastern culture that we tend to simplify and think of as being very repressive toward women actually has this wonderful fashion," she says. "Imagine women under burqas wearing this incredibly detailed and beautiful and ornate clothing."

Wilde's own style has evolved into a mix of her mother's classicism and world-traveling shopping habits, and her own flower-child impulses. For that school-bus wedding, she wore an antique silk scarf-turned-top and flowers in her hair. (Years later, looking at pictures, she realized she'd been so nervous at the time that the top was inside out.) Later, the couple made up for that modest ceremony twofold: first with a "Fitzgeraldian" black-tie party at

66I HAVE FUN WITH FASHION, BUT I'M NOT ONE OF THOSE GIRLS WHO SPEND HOURS A DAY OBSESSING OVER IT.99

OLIVIA

A passion since childhood: Exotic jewelry, which her journalist parents would bring back from South America, the Middle East, and Africa

Wilde lounges on the brocade couch in her dressing room, wearing an Equipment blouse and a 3.1 Phillip Lim skirt.

her parents' country house in Virginia horse country, after "one of those monsoon tropical thunderstorms passed through, so everything was bright green, and everyone was holding up their beautiful gowns as they walked through the muddy, grassy hills. It was just absolutely beautiful and raucous." And after that, there was yet another wedding party, this time at Ruspoli's family castle in Rome, complete with stilt walkers, violinists, and flag-bearers. "It was straight out of the Renaissance, the way weddings were performed there for hundreds of years," she says.

Soon after the wedding, they moved into this house in Venice—a major leap from their tiny tricked-out bus, which has since retired to "an old-folks' home for buses." Her first reaction to the imposing, modern steel structure? "Honestly, I couldn't see it. I was thinking, God, it looks really harsh and industrial...how about a little cottage on the canals?" she says. Ruspoli, who studied architecture at Berkeley before moving on to film, sold her: "He said, 'What about a great open space for making art and having parties and spilling things and not worrying?'" Wilde agreed, but not without softening the strict modern space with a hippie-fied touch: The night before they closed on the house, the couple broke in at midnight and stained the concrete floor with acid to create an ocean-green swirly effect. "We were so good at it, eventually the neighbors asked us to do theirs, too," says Wilde, laughing.

Wilde in her dressing room, wearing a Boy blazer, Derek Lam skirt, and vintage YSL sunglasses

With her husband, filmmaker Tao Ruspoli

FASHION FLASHBACK

Wilde stunned in Marchesa on the red carpet: "When I wore this dress to the Emmys in 2009, everyone was like, 'Wow, you're wild!' I thought it was just the most beautifully crafted thing I'd ever seen. It was like wearing a piece of art; it had all these large sections of sheer netting. I've always enjoyed the spectacle factor in wearing something like that, especially on the red carpet. You feel like you're performing."

HER FAVORITE SHOPS

VINTAGE FURNITURE AT OBSOLETE
obsoleteinc.com
222 Main Street
Venice, CA 90291
(310) 399-0024

TOMS SHOES AT FRED SEGAL FUN
500 Broadway
Santa Monica, CA 90401
(310) 394-9814

LNA T-SHIRTS AT CONFEDERACY
4661 Hollywood Boulevard
Los Angeles, CA 90027
(323) 913-3040

CAROL DEAN'S RESALE THERAPY
shopresaletherapy.com
4109 East Palm Canyon Drive
Palm Springs, CA 92264
(760) 321-6556

SHAREEN VINTAGE
350 North Avenue 21
Los Angeles, CA 90031
(323) 276-6226

STYLE STUDY

An easy peasant top brings Wilde's polished skirt down to earth.

She keeps it cool on the red carpet in a hippie-ish dress and flip flops.

Loads of embellishment keeps things interesting on this classic hourglass dress.

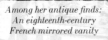

Among her antique finds: An eighteenth-century French mirrored vanity

Pages from Wilde's childhood photo albums

A vintage Panama hat gives any outfit a laid-back feel.

A stack of ethnic bangles says breezy beauty.

Toms slide-ons are supercool with shorts or a maxidress.

A wide scoop neck gives an Autumn Cashmere sweater easy elegance—the perfect match for wide-legged Levi's.

WILDE'S STYLE IS A PRODUCT OF HER ESOTERIC BACKGROUND AND OPEN MIND.

Wilde describes her closet as "a little private land" that doubles as a "therapy room" when advice-seeking friends come to visit—and it's got space for a crowd. Despite the well-stocked wardrobe, the actress's approach to dressing is resolutely low key. If she's riding her bike to get her morning coffee in Venice Beach, she'll opt for hippie jeans, an LnA T-shirt, and her slide-on Toms, "the most comfortable shoe in the world." If it's time to celebrate, Wilde opts for a long, flowing gown, as she did for her Fitzgerald-themed wedding party (one of three nuptial celebrations). No matter the scenery, the 26-year-old doesn't "obsess over fashion," but instead "appreciates it as an art form."

ESTELLE, PHOTOGRAPHED
IN HER NEW YORK CITY
HIGH-RISE APARTMENT.

Opposite: Her Best Rap/Sung
Collaboration Grammy for
"American Boy"

ESTELLE

SHAPE SHIFTER

OCCUPATION	*Singer, rapper*
BEST KNOWN FOR	*Crooning with Kanye West on the chart topper "American Boy"*
HOME BASE	*New York City*

THE ELLEMENTS OF ESTELLE

THE VIEW FROM Estelle's thirty-fifth-floor apartment—an unobstructed panorama of Manhattan's West Side, from midtown all the way down to the Statue of Liberty—could inspire a visitor to belt out the lyrics to "New York, New York." It seems an apt theme song (though slightly off genre) for this rapper-cum-singer, whose Motown-flavored romanticism, gritty rhymes, and dance-floor beats have earned comparisons to everyone from Amy Winehouse to Lauryn Hill. Can she, as Sinatra would croon, "make it there?" "American Boy," her toe-tapping, disco-flavored duet with rainmaker Kanye West, indicated that she most certainly can: The song jammed

> **❝I LIKE CLEAN, I LIKE SHARP, I LIKE LINES.❞**
>
> ESTELLE

Above and opposite: In dresses by a favorite designer, Bernard Chandran. Both are "perfect for when I perform."

airwaves for the better part of 2008—and in her window, overlooking that view, sits the Grammy to prove it.

Not that it's been easy. British critics have been proclaiming the West London native music's "next big thing" since 2004, when she made her mark with the autobiographical rap song

"1980"—a hit that she launched on her own, after waiting for years to be picked up by a label. "Pop starlets are a dime a dozen," says the singer, rarely one to pull a punch. "If you want to do something remotely credible, you have to fight and battle, battle and fight to get signed. All the stars have to be aligned. And I was sick of waiting for that to happen." Even with the buzzy success of "1980," it took a while for Estelle to find her groove in the industry; she was picked up by the recording company V2, on which she released her first album *The 18th Day*. But a coincidental run-in with on-the-rise Kanye West at L.A.'s Roscoe's House of Chicken and Waffles offered a real game-changing moment. She sauntered right up to West and asked him to introduce her to his friend John Legend (having no idea that Legend was, in fact, the guy sitting right next to him). The faux pas paid off: Legend eventually bought her out of her contract with V2 and, in 2008, her second album, *Shine*, became the first release on his own Home School Records imprint, a division of Atlantic.

The first of eight children, Estelle Swaray was raised by her Senegalese mother, a devout Christian who didn't allow secular music in the house, and her reggae-loving West Indian father. She grew up helping raise her siblings, and despite occasional financial straits, there was a wealth of culture: African food and gospel music, the slow grooves of Bob Marley, and, of course, the street influences of '80s London. So in addition to Ella Fitzgerald, Mary J. Blige, and Dinah Washington, Estelle ranks, tellingly, David Bowie, Guns N' Roses, and Freddie Mercury among her idols.

These are not the type of artists who get by on beauty and sheer sex appeal—they had a *look*. "Growing up, I wasn't a Whitney girl," Estelle says.

Behind the scenes of her Los Angeles-based video for "Freak"—a song "about letting out your inner freak."

"Whitney was fun, but the poodle perm? I just didn't get that. But I liked Grace Jones. It was in your face, and it was clean." And as far-out as Jones may have been, she was relatable: "I identified with her a little bit. She had a small nose, you know, small eyes. She resembled what I saw in the mirror. And I honestly couldn't tell if it was her or her brother at any given time." A tomboy until her mid-twenties, Estelle also idolized the spacey gender-bending outfits of Bowie and Annie Lennox. "That's what I grew up thinking of as sexy," she says. "The look is powerful."

So while she's not afraid to show off her two favorite assets, her cleavage and her legs, her closet—which, incidentally, occupies at least a third of the square footage in her high-rise abode—is full of clothes that are as challenging as her own hard-to-peg music. "I like clean, I like sharp, I like lines," says Estelle, whose onstage looks tend to have a touch of Judy Jetson: sparkly, hypermodern fabrics; asymmetrical necklines; and robotic silhouettes that emphasize her every move—one more element of showmanship. "Stuff like that changes the way you move; it changes your posture," she says. "It gives everything a whole new spin."

To wit: For the Grammys, where most stars struggle to either out-bling or out-sex their competition, she chose a sil-ver dress with fins jutting out over each hip by Malaysian designer Bernard Chandran, which would have fit right in had the awards ceremony been held on, say, Mars. "I was like, How the hell do you think to put freaking triangles on the sides of my hips?" she says, clearly delighted. "I felt like a sexy robot lady."

The luxury of designer robo-dresses and Nicholas Kirkwood shoes ("friggin' pieces of art," she says) is not lost on Estelle, who not so long ago was 18 years old and barely getting by—working all day, going out at night to do gigs, and doing it all in her one pair of shoes, which were Nikes. "I washed them and I wore them, and I washed them and I wore them," she says. "And I said, 'Once I start making money, I'm never, ever, *ever* going to have just one pair of shoes again.'" The day after she won her first award, for "1980," "I said, 'I'm going out to buy myself a good pair of shoes.'" But when she blithely handed the crystal-embellished green satin heels to the salesperson at Jimmy Choo, she panicked. "I was so mad at myself! I gave them my credit card before I could take it back," she says, laughing. "I cried. I wanted them, but they were £800!" Now, although she proudly proclaims, "I have a trillion pairs," those Jimmy Choos will have a special place in her story forever.

INSPIRATION BOARD

FASHION FLASHBACK

In 2004 Estelle celebrated her first big success by splurging on these crystal-encrusted emerald Jimmy Choos. "I just spent £800 on a pair of shoes! I'll never give them away."

In her closet—the guitar she's learning to play

The headgear in her guest-room-cum-dressing room: Wigs, plus dozens of scarves, sunglasses, and hats; below left: Performing "American Boy" with West at the Grammy Awards in 2009

Left: A crisp blazer and a sexy spectator pump put a new spin on R&B sex appeal. "I find this androgynous look really sexy—it feels assertive."

Estelle's style icons, from left: Grace Jones, Freddie Mercury, Axl Rose, Annie Lennox, Billie Holiday, and David Bowie

Estelle 101: statement-making shapes in vibrant, shimmery fabrics

A waist-defining Azzedine Alaïa belt looks futuristic in black patent.

If an outlandish dress isn't quite your speed, try a pointy-shouldered Balmain jacket. Decorated with chains? Even better.

Nicholas Kirkwood's architectural shoes could double as interior decor.

A bold Louis Vuitton choker and Jetsons-worthy Stella McCartney cuff adds a dash of futurism.

ONSTAGE AND OFF, ESTELLE DARES TO CHALLENGE R&B'S STYLE STATUS QUO.

For Estelle, androgynous separates and transforming silhouettes are paramount. The singer might conjure Grace Jones or David Bowie by performing in an "assertive" menswear-inspired shirt-and-tie ensemble, or channel the supergalactic style of the late Queen frontman Freddie Mercury. She jokes she's been on "the eternal search" to find her waist with figure-defining belts, and "collects shoes like they're pieces of art," stocking her closet with outlandish heels from the likes of Charlotte Olympia and Brit designer Nicholas Kirkwood. Onstage she relies on her ensemble to perform one task: "It's gotta scream, 'I know what I'm doing!'"

VILLAREAL, PHOTOGRAPHED IN
FRONT OF A LIGHT SCULPTURE
THAT CHANGES COLOR
THROUGHOUT THE DAY
BY HER HUSBAND, LEO.

Yvonne

YVONNE FORCE VILLAREAL

ART-WORLD SWIRL

OCCUPATION	*Cofounder of Art Production Fund*
BEST KNOWN FOR	*Facilitating groundbreaking public art*
HOME BASE	*West Village, New York City*

THE ELLEMENTS OF YVONNE

WHENEVER New York City's fashion world collides with its contemporary art scene, you'll likely spot a certain cool blond in head-to-toe Dolce & Gabbana. That's Yvonne Force Villareal. Villareal has a laser-sharp eye for talent and a knack for making "happenings" happen. In 1996 she and architect Doreen Remen set out to help artist-on-the-verge Vanessa Beecroft, who was "piecemeal-ing her shows together," says Villareal. "We thought maybe we could help her create a really *ideal* performance." The result, *Show,* involved 20 women—five stark naked, the rest in slivers of red rhinestone bikinis designed by Tom Ford for Gucci—standing in stark rows in the Guggenheim, looking simultaneously tough and vulnerable. It was free, open to the public, and big: it landed on the cover of *Artforum.* That marked the start of Art Production Fund, Remen and Villareal's nonprofit,

Masterpieces by six-year-old son, Cuatro; *opposite:* In an Yves Saint Laurent dress in front of a Martin Eder painting

which facilitates public art, including the Electric Fountain, a 30-ton light sculpture by Sue Webster and Tim Noble in the middle of Rockefeller Center; and Prada Marfa, a faux boutique in the middle of the Texas desert by the artists Elmgreen & Dragset.

ELLE: You had a nomadic childhood.

Yvonne Force Villareal: We lived in several places, but mostly I grew up in a 24-by-8-foot trailer in Key West, Florida. My mother raised me and my sister, and my older brother was an officer in the Navy nearby. It was truly bohemian. We had no television. There were artists around all the time, musicians. I grew up barefoot in a bikini, and I drew obsessively.

ELLE: What's your first vivid fashion memory?

YFV: The three of us would go to a store called Under the Banyan Tree for custom-made matching bathing suits. One was burnt orange with chocolate-brown trim. I also had a stars-and-stripes suit for the naval swim team. The sun would go through the white stars, and I'd have tan stars on my body.

ELLE: By 1984 you were a New York City nightclub regular.

YFV: [The club] AREA was amazing. I was a young soon-to-be art student, and here were the icons—Andy Warhol, Grace Jones. My general look was the same thing I still do now: superpale lips, dark eyes, tight pants, high heels. Big jackets, big men's overcoats. I had an asymmetric haircut—a long bob with one side slightly shorter—and everything teased. And I didn't go anywhere without shoulder pads. I put them into everything.

ELLE: How do you decide which pieces of art to bring home?

YFV: I have to have an absolute intuitive feeling, a connection to it. There's so much work I love, but I don't want to necessarily live with it. It has to

have a real dialogue with the other pieces around it.

ELLE: How often do you go to openings and events?

YFV: About three times a week. Before my son [Cuatro, age six, with sculptor husband Leo Villareal], I used to go out every night. Sundays I never go out, ever.

ELLE: There are an awful lot of yoga mats in your house.

YFV: We have a grassroots community-yoga project. We host about five practices a week. For me it's really a spiritual practice. I'm working on becoming more conscious, more awake, aware, appreciative, and intuitive.

ELLE: You have a wardrobe trick to accommodate this personal growth.

YFV: I've been wearing catsuits since RISD. Whatever you have on over one, you can just take off and get right on the mat. Also, it's black and tight, like a body stocking, so you feel smooth and comfortable. I'd wear it by itself if I had more nerve.

ELLE: How do you take that from day to night?

YFV: To work, I wear it with a long V-neck cashmere sweater and pink ballet flats and, say, a Prada raincoat. At night, I'd put on high, high boots, take off the sweater, and tie the raincoat tight. Open the collar and roll up the sleeves, so it becomes like a little dress. Put on black, thick eyeliner, tease my hair a little bit, and maybe add a choker.

ELLE: Do you dress for the art you're going to see?

YFV: Absolutely. For a Wolfgang Tillmans opening—interesting work that's not so highly formal—I'd definitely have a more grungy, young look. For a Philip Taaffe opening at the Gagosian, a structured cocktail dress. That's part of the theater of it. Clothes help make sense of how you're feeling.

Villareal relaxes in the tub beside a Keith Edmier sculpture; her pomeranian, Puff Baby, keeps watch below.

YVONNE'S WORLD

"This sculpture by Peter Coffin just stood out at Art Basel—I had to live with it. I love how it appears to have just landed on a pedestal and closed its eyes while facing the wall."

"Rachel Feinstein made this for our son, Cuatro— she creates biographical sculptures for her close friends that have babies. It's Don Quixote on a horse on top of a number four."

Lisa Yuskavage's *Blonde, Brunette and Redhead* triptych overlooks a Milo Baughman dining set found on eBay. *Below:* A slouchy '70s couch in bubblegum pink

Wearing Dolce & Gabbana over one of her onesie staples on a John Chamberlain draped sofa

A portrait of friend Rachel Feinstein, by Feinstein's husband, John Currin, hangs in the guest bathroom.

INSPIRATION BOARD

An Art Production Fund project: *Prada Marfa (2005), a faux boutique in the Texan desert*

FOR VILLAREAL, FASHION AND ART ARE A PERFECT MATCH.

Whether she's helping artists and designers collaborate, or lending her colorful presence—in white go-go boots, chokers, and Dolce & Gabbana party dresses—to a gallery opening, there's always a bit of fashion in whatever Villareal does. Asked if her style has changed much over the years, she replies: "I don't want to tone it down. I'm a girl who wants to have a fun time dressing."

HER FAVORITE SHOPS

DANCEWEAR SOLUTIONS
dancewearsolutions.com
6730 Manchester Avenue
St. Louis, MO 63139
(314) 754-1948

DONNA KARAN, URBAN ZEN
donnakaran.com
urbanzen.org
705 Greenwich St.
New York, NY 10014
(212) 206-3999

OPENING CEREMONY
openingceremony.us
35 Howard Street
New York, NY 10013
(212) 219-2688

ELISE ØVERLAND
eliseoverland.com
601 West 26th Street
New York, NY 10001
(212) 239-4004

STYLE STUDY

A shimmery, slouchy top takes her standard unitard out on the town.

A pop of bare shoulder and nude pumps keep head-to-toe black ultrasexy.

Villareal gets a kick out of going totally over-the-top—like this cotton-candy-colored fur.

Performing at a Fendi party with her friend Sandra Hamburg as ironic rap-pop duo Mother, Inc.

6. I collect ___ART___ because:
Artists offer alternative perspectives and possibilities in their work.

15. When I fell in love I was wearing:
My husband fell in love with my boots first, then with me! The ubiquitous Tomford, Gucci, Black Patent leather, 3/4 calf!

"I WEAR A FANTASTIC LYCRA JUMPSUIT UNDER ALMOST ALL OF MY CLOTHES."

YVONNE

Whether she pairs them with Dolce & Gabbana sequins or a Stella McCartney blazer, Villareal's catsuits have been at the foundation of her look for decades.

MISSONI, PHOTOGRAPHED AT
HER FAMILY COMPOUND IN
SUMIRAGO, ITALY

Opposite: Two Missoni knits, fresh off
the factory floor

MARGHERITA MISSONI

JET-SET GYPSY

OCCUPATION	*Missoni Brand Ambassador and Accessories Designer*
BEST KNOWN FOR	*Acting as the face of the fashion dynasty*
HOME BASE	*Sumirago, Italy*

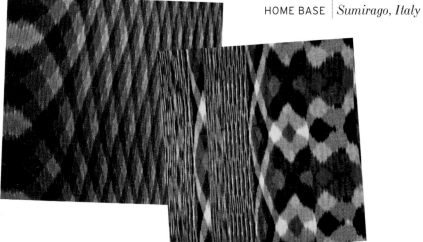

THE ELLEMENTS OF MARGHERITA

A S A CHILD, Margherita Missoni assumed that all kids came home from school and went straight into their ateliers to play with dolls, yarn, and scraps of fabric. "It never occurred to me that it was something different to have your own fashion company," says Missoni, her voice—deep and slightly growly, like that of an old-school Italian screen goddess— a sexy contrast to her fresh-faced looks.

In the '50s, '60s, and '70s, Ottavio and Rosita (that's Grandma and Grandpa to Margherita) wove their slinky, dizzying zigzags and stripes in a mélange of colors never before seen— or at least never in such joyous profusion. Theirs was Italian style—all glorious color and superluxe quality—but remixed with a lush, laid-back bohemian flavor that was 100 percent Missoni. And *famiglia* was always foremost: In 1969, when it was time to build a headquarters, Ottavio and Rosita situated the factory 30 miles outside of Milan, among woods, cornfields, and their other passion, a garden. Eventually, they built homes for their kids on the property, including Angela (who took over designing for the family business in 1996) and her children, Margherita, now 27; Francesco, 25; and Teresa, 22.

In her twenties, Margherita moved from Rome to Paris to New York, studying acting and jetting around the globe as the company's "ambassador," hosting fragrance launches and boutique openings while wearing her mother's designs, always with her own romantic spin. "I like to dress up," she says, wrinkling her nose at what she calls *American casual*. "I think dressing up should be brought back into fashion." When she throws parties, she likes to set a dress code—though some guests were surely flummoxed by the theme of her recent birthday party, "polka-dot Jamaican tuxedo." Missoni, of course, had just the thing: a vintage backless Norma Kamali gown in black with yellow, green, and red polka dots.

It was only a matter of time before the Missoni genetic imperative— design!—caught up with her. She started with sunglasses but soon moved back home to focus full time on bags, swimwear, and, it seems, an around-the-clock roster of design

Knit wits: Margherita, left, snuggles up with her sister, Teresa, at the family estate. *Right:* The clan in full Missoni regalia

responsibilities. The temporary move back to her childhood bedroom after years on her own was trying, she admits, but "I have a drive to do this that I never had for anything. For me, fashion, my family—it's always been difficult to separate. [The company] is something that's your own; you really feel a pride about it, and you wouldn't want anyone to do anything wrong to it."

There seems to be no question as to whether she has what it takes to design; her own wardrobe, after all, has been the subject of international fascination for years. Missoni collects lingerie—vintage and new, from Kiki de Montparnasse froth to Hanro classic cotton—men's shirts, clunky boots by Martin Margiela, and ornamented heels from Balenciaga. Though the foundation of her look is "Missoni, always Missoni!" she also "supports the industry" (that's fashion-speak for voracious shopping), snapping up fresh-off-the-runway looks from Alaïa, Prada, Alexander Wang, Zac Posen, and Yves Saint Laurent.

In fact, all three generations of Missoni women are born shoppers. "We buy so much junk—you have no idea!" she laughs. When she was growing up, the Missoni womenfolk's favorite Sunday activity was trawling flea markets and accumulating dishware, furniture, and an odd array of ephemera. Missoni, whose first name means "daisy" in Italian, has a collection of the naive flowers, and another of fish in honor of her Pisces sign—"any excuse to start a collection," she says. And the house became even more overstuffed recently, when Angela discovered eBay and bought a mini laptop just for tracking her finds. "She's on it virtually every hour she's awake," says her daughter. "I'm like, 'You have it on *again*?' and she says, 'Just one thing! It's going to expire in a minute!'" They offload the excess at a friend's antiques shop or re-list the items online—"Some maniac will buy it," says Missoni, knowingly.

In the Missoni clan, the passing of the torch seems to happen with relative ease, and Margherita seems clearly poised to take on the mantle. "My grandmother told me, 'When I was younger, even if I wasn't really someone who liked going to clubs, I'd go to Studio 54 just to see what was going on.' She was curious to go see things, to sleep four hours, to go to a flea market and be the first one there—which is exactly how I feel right now," says Missoni. "But at one point, she didn't feel that anymore. She realized she had to step back, because she wasn't curious about it anymore."

Should the granddaughter, now utterly fashion obsessed, ever reach a similar ennui, she'll have a ready-made refuge. Semi-retirement, after all, is another thing Missonis do especially well. Rosita and Ottavio still spend two to three hours a day in the garden: She tends the fruits and vegetables and picks mushrooms and greens for their daily salads; he nurses the flowers. "They have plants that grow on top of plants," says Missoni. "And there's always a flower that blooms, every month." There's also a chicken coop and a rabbit hutch and, in the nearby town, a coin-operated pump that fills glass bottles with fresh milk from the local dairy farms, and—oh, yeah—a rather haute fashion company, right on the premises.

> **66 HALF OF MY MEMORIES OF GROWING UP ARE FROM THE FACTORY. IT'S REALLY FUN FOR A KID—EVERY TYPE OF PAPER, COLOR, PAINT, AND FABRIC TO STITCH ON. 99**
>
> MARGHERITA

Opposite: Missoni in Missoni, on the factory floor; *above:* Hair ornaments and ethnic jewelry complete her Boho charm.

MARGHERITA'S WORLD

"You pick up ideas wherever you go, wherever you look. That's why it's so important to be in an inspiring environment. If you always see the same gray wall, you're going to pick up on that."

Missoni Home riotous patterned carpets

A painting by Tancredi;
the deco vases were gifts
from Paris' Porte de Vanves;
right: Fabrics in development

The company's
iconic zigzag, first
introduced circa 1966

INSPIRATION BOARD

FOLLOW MISSONI'S LEAD: RAID THE BOUDOIR FOR PARTY-PRETTY PIECES.

Whether it's vintage lacy tanks borrowed from her mother or bold pieces from current designers, Missoni turns delicate camisoles and silky dressing gowns into eveningwear.

An iconic Missoni print

Rosita Missoni en famiglia. "My approach to style is never too matchy—that definitely comes from my grandmother," says Margherita.

STYLE STUDY

Missoni makes a midriff top elegant with relaxed sultan pants.

To put a twist on her usual bohemian vibe, Missoni adds a cool gaucho hat.

For parties, the designer sticks to a winning formula: floor-length dresses in the family prints.

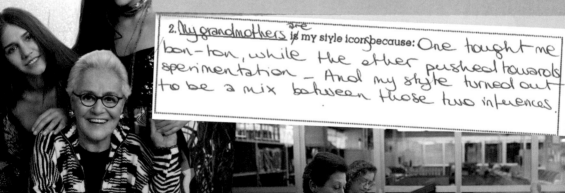

2. My grandmothers is my style icons because: One tought me bon-ton, while the other pushed towards sperimentation — And my style turned out to be a mix between those two inferences.

Missoni's fashion icons: The original jet-set bohemian, Talitha Getty, and the eccentric heiress Marchesa Luisa Casatti (left)

4. The most reliable thing in my closet:

A chanel tweed mini skirt.

11. I'd never change my:

Eyebrows, breasts and sense of humor.

HER FAVORITE SHOPS

NEW YORK VINTAGE
117 West 25th Street
New York, NY 10001
(212) 647-1107

THE WAY WE WORE
334 S. La Brea Avenue
Los Angeles, CA 90036
(323) 937-0878

MISSONI
8 Via Montenapoleone
Milan, Italy
+39-2-76-00-35-55

PRADA
8 Via Montenapoleone
Milan, Italy
+39-2-76-02-40-12

1. My most prized possession:
A 1950s cheeta coat that belonged to my greataunt

16. The piece that changed my life: American Apparel stretch, short sleeve, cotton, mini dress; the first short and tight thing I ever wore. It changed my whole approach to dressing. Only after that I felt confident enough to wear body hugging ALAIAs

Whether it's actual lingerie or a lacy retro-inspired shift, a slinky, body-skimming dress forms a sexy wardrobe foundation.

Hippie-fied chains and wide-leg Etro trousers, two Missoni staples

Marc Jacobs' eclectic woven bag is a perfect match for Margherita's signature jewel-box palette.

Pointy shoes? Too aggressive for Missoni, who prefers stacked heels with an open or round toe.

BLENDING FAMILY HEIRLOOMS WITH TOUCHES OF RICH TEXTURE, MISSONI'S LOOK REFLECTS HER GLAMOROUS WORLD.

Missoni mixes her family's signature zigzags with lingerie collected at vintage stores and off-the-beaten-path shops, romantic round-toe high heels, decadent cropped furs, and flowing bohemian dresses that have an inherent carefree ease. Never one to be "matchy," she mixes button-downs from the Missoni Men collection with chunky sweaters for workdays at the family HQ, and Yves Saint Laurent platforms with slinky Missoni slipdresses for society events. No matter the combination, the designer always aims to capture—as her grandmother and mother long have—*l'air du temps.*

❝EVERY GIRL SHOULD OWN A MISSONI BIKINI!❞

MARGHERITA

Whether it's the real McCoy or a similarly bohemian print, a richly patterned swimsuit will make you look like
you're yacht-hopping on the Riviera—whether you're Mediterranean-bound or not.

POPE, PHOTOGRAPHED AT
HER SANTA MONICA OFFICE
WEARING BOTTEGA VENETA.

Opposite: Pope as a toddler

KATHERINE POPE

PARED-DOWN PRACTICAL

OCCUPATION	*TV producer*
BEST KNOWN FOR	*Helping create hit shows such as* 30 Rock, Heroes, *and* House M.D.
HOME BASE	*Hancock Park, Los Angeles*

STANDING AT THE head of the boardroom in her new Santa Monica, California, office, wearing a figure-hugging Bottega Veneta purple dress, Katherine Pope looks like the sexy-serious star of a courtroom drama. *L.A. Law*, the spinoff, perhaps? Hardly. She may be a dead ringer for Jennifer Connelly, but Pope is no starlet. As the head of television for Chernin Entertainment, she's one of a handful of people in this town who can get courtroom dramas, among other things, made.

At any given time, Pope, 37, oversees 30 TV shows in development, a load that sounds inhuman but to her "is like a cakewalk." Just three years ago, having bounded rapidly up the corporate ladder at NBC, Pope was appointed president of NBC Universal Media Studios, where she looked after some 25 shows in production and 80 projects in development. A few of these were flops—*Lipstick Jungle, My Own Worst Enemy*—but other pet projects became some of the biggest shows on TV: *House M.D., Heroes, 30 Rock*. In late 2008, with NBC in upheaval, she was unceremoniously dumped ("I cried," she says. "But not at work!"), but within eight months had signed on at this new enterprise,

which is helmed by Peter Chernin, the former head of 20th Century Fox and the Fox network. Her new role is tough, she says: "You've got to be scrappier, you have to push harder, you have to continue to work on stuff even when you get the sense that maybe it's not going forward."

Pope is a deck-stacker; at the moment, she's not just starting a new job and moving into a new office, she's also doing a top-to-bottom renovation of her house. "While it's happening, I'll be like, Oh my God, why did I do that? I'm so crazy!" she says. "But if I have nothing going on, it's, Well, that's kind of boring; let's do something else." She's known in the business for being unpretentious, funny, charming—but no pushover. "I'm not an insecure person," she says. "I don't worry about being liked." When it's time to fire someone, she doesn't hesitate, and, though she laments the shortage of female mentors in her field, she's blunt about the drawbacks of some female colleagues: "Chicks can be annoying at work."

Shifting from job to job at NBC, Pope had a running joke: "I was like, I wonder which white guy I'm going to answer to now," she says, laughing. Time and again, she was told, "Don't get hysterical" and "You have to mature; you're too emotional." Slight of

Right: A college-age Pope, looking more like a future movie star than a future exec; *above:* Heading to work in a Burberry trench; *opposite:* With daughter Willa in the Versace dress she wore to the 2010 Academy Awards

> **THE WORK THAT I DO IS INTENSELY INTIMATE AND PERSONAL. IF YOU'RE GOING TO ASK A WRITER TO REVEAL SOME PART OF THEMSELVES, YOU'VE GOT TO BE PREPARED TO REVEAL SOME PART OF YOURSELF, TOO.**

KATHERINE

build, pretty, and looking even younger than her age, she would suit up for meetings in the fifty-second-floor boardroom at 30 Rock (the real-life NBC HQ, after which the show is named), but "I think they always thought of me as a little bit of a girl," she says. "I felt a bit that way, too, like I was playing at my dad's office. It's not just that you're the only woman in the room, which I often was, but you're kind of the only *girl* in the room."

It was in one of those moments that Pope came to appreciate power dressing. She was asked to make a presentation on an upcoming season for the whole company, plus, "like, 5,000 Wall Street analysts," she laughs. "I went up there wearing a skirt I had bought at Club Monaco in 1996. It's a pencil skirt—it's classic, I love it. But in my head, I was thinking, Seriously, Club Monaco...1996?" As a brainy kid from the wealthy suburb of Glencoe, Illinois, who had done a stint at the elite Miss Porter's prep school, Pope was resolutely low-maintenance. (Indeed,

flipping through pictures dating back to her school days, she laughs: "See? Nothing has changed!") She didn't overspend on clothes and had long been able to "take a shower, put my wet hair in a bun, and go to work." But in that moment, she realized that wasn't going to cut it anymore. She and her assistant hightailed it to Saks. "I needed some real clothes," she says.

Her five-year-old daughter, Willa, is the clotheshorse in Pope's household; she arrived at our shoot in mini Uggs, chattering about the afternoon's planned shopping excursion, and gleefully jumped into model poses for our photographer as Pope and her husband of nine years, documentary filmmaker Richard E. Robbins, looked on in bemused awe.

Getting out the door in the morning "is sometimes like storming the beach at Normandy. Go! Go! Go!" Pope says. The goal is to look put-together in a matter of minutes. Though she laughs when put on the spot about defining her personal style, Pope has a well-defined look. Even when she invested in "real" clothes in order to look (and feel) like a woman in charge, she didn't sacrifice an ounce of femininity; she never chopped off her still-girlish hair or invested in ill-suited statement clothes. She sticks to diamond studs and well-tailored LBDs and can execute a shopping trip, start to finish, in about 15 minutes. "My joke is, if I'm going to a fancy party, maybe the black dress is designer—Prada or Dolce & Gabbana—and maybe the diamond earrings are bigger," she says. "Adding red lipstick: That's me stepping it up."

"Instead of just playing the victim of the working mom—the 'I can't be every place at once' sort of thing—I think, It's my choice, and my life can look however I want it to look."

INSPIRATION BOARD

15. When I fell in love I was wearing:
- Bad hair
- Big bottoms
- Chunky heels
- Tiny miniskirt

14. I've spent a whole paycheck on:
- YSL BOOTS
- Prada (everything)
- Cashmere ~~sweaters~~
- Hotels

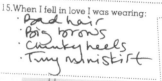

At her 2001 wedding, wearing Vera Wang and Manolo Blahnik: "My shoes cost more than my dress!"

5. I feel most beautiful when: I'm on day 3 of a week-long beach vacation. A little sandy, a little sunny and totally at peace.

POPE'S STREAMLINED APPROACH TO DRESSING IS BOARDROOM-POLISHED BUT NEVER STUFFY.

Pope has distilled a clean-lined style that works day in and day out, and makes getting it right every morning a snap. Her office uniform consists of shapely, well-cut "pencil skirts and little black dresses," paired with classic stilettos and a cardigan. Day-to-night transformations are easy: simply add red lipstick.

HER FAVORITE SHOPS

J.CREW
Jcrew.com

SAKS FIFTH AVENUE
611 Fifth Avenue
New York, NY 10022
(212) 753-4000

PHILOSOPHY DI ALBERTA FERRETTI
452 West Broadway
New York, NY 10012
(212) 460-5500

BERGDORF GOODMAN SHOE SALON
754 Fifth Avenue
New York, NY 10019
(212) 753-7300

STYLE STUDY

A classic strapless gown in a deep opulent hue is a Pope essential.

This well-cut shift can quick-change from office to eveningwear.

In this electric-pink shift, Pope is just as glam as Heroes star Ali Larter.

2. My daughter is my style icon because: She has been totally decisive about her taste since she was born — I may not love color as much as she does, but I admire her style courage.

9. People compliment my:
- insane work ethic
- insanely fast blackberry typing
- ability to seem tall (even though I'm not)
- hair (when I brush it)
- → No one has ever complimented my driving (it's awful)

Photographed by her husband in the mid-'90s

"I HAVE TWO PAIRS OF DIAMOND STUDS THAT I WEAR ALL THE TIME."

KATHERINE

With a look as simple and elegant as Pope's, every nuance counts. Here, Tiffany studs and a slash of red lipstick are all it takes to finish off a classic shift dress.

VON TEESE, PHOTOGRAPHED IN THE BEDROOM OF HER HOLLYWOOD HOME.

Opposite: A second-grade portrait of little Dita, aka Heather Sweet

Dita

DITA VON TEESE

PINUP PRECISION

OCCUPATION	*Burlesque performer*
BEST KNOWN FOR	*Making a fashion statement, whether putting clothes on or taking them off*
HOME BASE	*Hollywood, Los Angeles*

WHAT COULD be more Hollywood than a major transformation? Rita Hayworth was born Margarita Carmen Cansino, a brunette Brooklynite who lacked the widow's peak that eventually became Hayworth's beauty trademark. Joan Crawford started out as a lowly chorus girl named Lucille Fay LeSueur. And Marilyn, as everybody knows, was once a bubbly strawberry blond named Norma Jean. Almost half a century later, a snub-nosed, freckly blond named Heather Sweet grew up in Rochester, Michigan, swooning over old movies and dreaming of her own Big Hollywood Makeover.

"When I looked in the mirror, I saw a blond girl with pale skin and no *color.* I wanted to be more colorful," says the woman now known as Dita Von Teese, who reignited the long-forgotten art of burlesque with her lustrous black hair, red lips, and to-the-letter retro wardrobe (and her knack for taking it off). Von Teese is beloved by men, of course, but she says most of her fans are women—and they're more interested in learning how she maintains her perfect coif (ladies, she colors it herself) than in her *Playboy* pics. Von Teese says she's not just trying to dust off the oldies; she'd like to open the door to another kind of beauty: "Look. I look stupid

with a tan, and I can never fit into that Gisele version of sexy. I'm trying to show people another way."

She says all this while perched on a plump green velvet couch in her completely retrofitted Los Angeles bungalow, looking like an exact replica of Hedy Lamarr: doll-like makeup, smooth curls, embroidered satin kimono. Von Teese's version of beauty may be different from the norm, but in today's jeans-and-lip-balm culture, it's not exactly accessible. In person, she is soft-spoken and so utterly ladylike—*demure,* to use a term from an era she might prefer—it's difficult to believe she rose to fame splashing around onstage in a bathtub-size martini glass (never mind the fact that she was once married to shock-rocker Marilyn Manson).

But there is something rather modern about this transformation story: the Svengali isn't some maniacal, sepia-tone studio boss—it's Dita herself. Von Teese prides herself on the work that has gone into creating and maintaining her own myth; she's proud that it requires an attention to detail that verges on "psycho." The precision with which she chooses her stockings (fully fashioned and nylon, not silk—"if I wore anything different, the real burlesque fans would know"); her strict, below-the-knee hemlines; and her preferred perky 1940s style and size of hat also informs every nuance of her shows. Whether she's climbing aboard a horse-size lipstick bullet or mincing about in $5 million worth of diamonds (or just some strategically placed bubbles), "it's my

Von Teese, wearing a custom Christian Lacroix dress made for the post-ceremony festivities at her 2005 wedding to Marilyn Manson, in her time-capsule living room—the walls were painted to match the turquoise of her favorite Burberry dress. "I knew it was a color I looked good in," she says. *Opposite:* "I'm really funny about the proportion of a hat—that kind of drives me to madness. Most are either too small or too big."

❝ I HAVE REALLY STRONG IDEAS ABOUT WHAT I WANT TO LOOK LIKE. WHEN OTHER PEOPLE GIVE ME THEIR OPINION, I USUALLY DO THE OPPOSITE.❞

DITA

production. I directed, produced, financed, choreographed, styled it. I ordered around the builders; I chose the paint colors—I did it," she says and then delivers a line straight out of a '40s movie: "It's not like anybody else is going to go to all the trouble to make some girl a star."

These days, Von Teese owns more dresses, jewelry, hats, stockings, bags, and shoes than she can count—including dozens of pairs of Louboutins, made just for her, that exist nowhere else on Earth. (One pair even has her name embroidered on the platform sole.) Her taste in vintage began in high school, as a matter of economics. "I would look at magazines and lust after Vivienne Westwood and John Galliano, but I couldn't afford them," she says. "I went to a vintage store and thought, Oh, I can make that look like a Westwood if I pinch in the waist and pad out the hips. That was my goal—to get that look for less."

She started with vintage lingerie—bullet bras, girdles, and '50s slips—repurposed as outerwear à la early-'90s Madonna. Working in the L.A. strip-club scene, she wore red lipstick and cat-eye liner—"I've worn the same makeup since I was allowed to wear makeup"—teased her long, blond hair into a beehive, and chose a new name (after Dita Parlow, a Jazz Age burlesque performer).

At this point, the alter ego is the genuine article. The only people who call her Heather are family members, and insecurities strike only when she's stripped of her fantastic plumage. "There have been a few times in my career when people have tried to 'undo' me, to take away everything that makes me feel sexy and good about myself, like the red lips and the eye liner and the heavy lashes and the right clothes," she says. "That's when I don't feel sexy at all. I feel stripped and naked and insecure." (And incognito: When one fashion designer asked her to walk his runway without her customary hair and makeup, no one in the audience recognized her.)

Her closet, she says, is a refuge of daily transformation. "My favorite thing about dressing is when you put something on and everything changes," she says. "The way you walk, your mannerisms, the way you look at people. I feel like my whole persona changes depending on my outfit." That's why she doesn't own a single pair of jeans. "That persona? It's too easy."

> ❝IN THE BEGINNING, I ALWAYS THOUGHT THE 'DITA' PERSONA WAS A HOBBY, SOMETHING FOR FUN. I THOUGHT I'D BE MARRIED WITH KIDS BY NOW.❞
>
> DITA

Opposite: "It's funny how people really listen to what you're saying when they have red lips pointed at them." *Above:* Even Von Teese's bathroom has matching retro curtains, wallpaper, and chandelier.

Performing in 2008 at the Angel Orensanz Foundation in New York City

Working the L.A. strip club scene, Dita borrowed a moniker from Jazz Age burlesque performer Dita Parlow

DITA'S WORLD

Wearing one of her favorites, a pristine 1954 Dior "New Look" suit. She turned the guest room into a hot-pink-walled treasure trove with hats and jewels on display.

Vintage '40s floral wallpaper in the dining room, with her childhood self looking on; *left:* Von Teese still does her own hair and makeup. One thing she can't live without: hot rollers

Von Teese has three Devon Rex cats—this one is perched on a velvet-covered '40s-repro couch in the living room. *Below:* Black lacquer drawers hold countless bags, piles of lingerie, and her stocking collection.

Idols on hand: Her hallway is lined with framed pictures of bygone starlets.

Among the ephemera, a refurbished '50s chandelier found at L.A.'s Antique Artistry (note the red ceiling); *below:* Vintage glassware

FASHION OBSESSION

With her stunning collection of heels, Von Teese just might be Christian Louboutin's best customer. Von Teese has a special relationship with the designer, who creates versions of his coveted red-soled heels for her performances and keeps a wooden mold of her foot at his workshop in Paris.

For Von Teese, burlesque isn't about serious seduction; her act is playful, light, witty—inspired by the camp innocence of acts from the '40s, '50s, and '60s, seen in these gems from her vintage pinup collection.

BEAUTY PARADE
The World's Loveliest Girls

WINK
A Fresh Magazine

Adam
1962 CALENDAR
the man's home companion!

20. Always: *ignore the critics... only mediocrity is safe from ridicule.*
Dare to be different!

17. My secret weapon:

I always enjoyed dressing like a femme-fatale to keep "easily intimidated" men from approaching me.

6. I collect Vintage because:

I am fascinated by the elegance of the past, and I love the thrill of the 'bargain hunt... plus it suits me.

7. My lifesaving beauty product:

My hot rollers... I could live without makeup, but straight hair is out of the question for me!

Technicolor dream girls: Teese's muses include, from top, Hedy Lamarr, Betty Grable, and Carmen Miranda.

STYLE STUDY

Von Teese admires the individualist ethos of women like the late, great fashion editor Diana Vreeland (below).

Red nails and lips keep her dove-gray dress and fair skin from fading into the background.

This dress is ultramodern, but the cut gives her curves classic definition.

Opera-length leather gloves add an elegant naughtiness to a cropped-sleeve coat.

Dear Joe

Love Dita

FASHION AND ACCESSORIES

Coy, flirty 3.1 Phillip Lim lingerie embodies Von Teese's sly take on burlesque.

With its '40s silhouette—nipped waist; narrow, below-the-knee skirt—this Christian Dior dress is a gateway to retro chic (even though it's not vintage).

Von Teese's daytime look is strictly covered-up and almost prim; pair this Carolina Herrera blouse with a pencil skirt and you're perfectly polished.

Every detail counts: Over-the-elbow Jil Sander opera gloves and a Prada brooch will up the elegance of any shift dress.

Evening news: A crystal-studded Judith Lieber clutch and red-trimmed Christian Louboutin heel

VON TEESE'S APPETITE FOR PERFECTION REFLECTS AN ENDURING LOVE AFFAIR WITH BYGONE GLAMOUR.

Star quality aside, being Dita Von Teese is all in the retro-inspired details: the raven hair, the alabaster skin, the ruby-red lips, and, of course, the signature hourglass silhouette. Whether it's the hand-stitched, seamed silk stockings the performer has made especially for her in France, designer Roland Mouret's black Galaxy dress (Von Teese admittedly "bought several at once"), or the sexy spike of a Louboutin heel, the performer's look is more than the sum of its parts. Von Teese advocates "building your own glamorous life," which she stresses one doesn't need money to achieve—just a certain "degree of craziness" for Old Hollywood polish.

"I NEVER FOCUS ON TRYING TO BE SEXY, JUST ON WHAT MAKES ME FEEL GOOD ABOUT MYSELF—THE LIPSTICK, THE STOCKINGS, THE HIGH HEELS."

DITA

Even when the majority of Von Teese's clothes are *off*—at least when she's onstage—you'll never catch her without her signature stem-wear. The footwear doesn't have to be Christian Louboutin but it does have to be sky-high and ladylike.

MARA, PHOTOGRAPHED
AT HOME IN HANCOCK
PARK, LOS ANGELES.

Opposite (from top): Evidence of the
family business on display in her
apartment; at seven, with her older
brother Danny, nine, during the
Giants' Super Bowl win in 1990

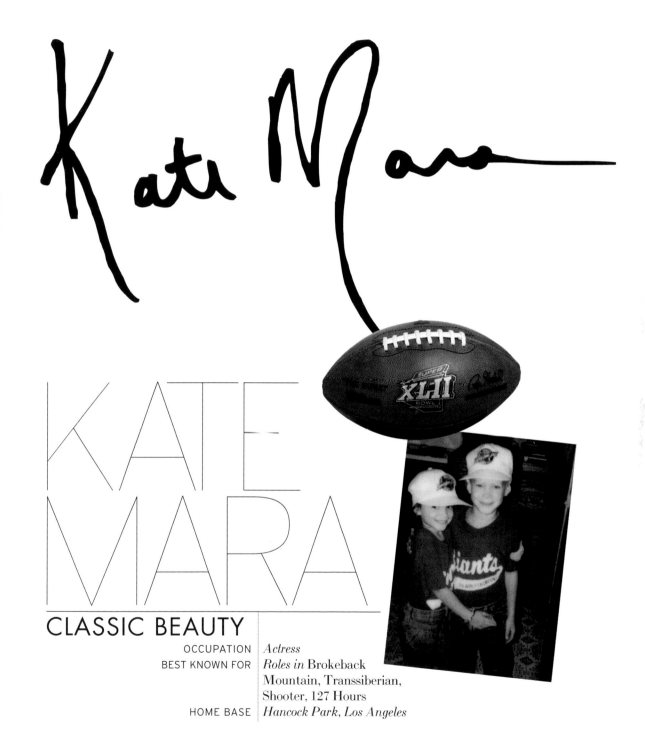

Kate Mara

KATE MARA

CLASSIC BEAUTY

OCCUPATION	*Actress*
BEST KNOWN FOR	*Roles in* Brokeback Mountain, Transsiberian, Shooter, 127 Hours
HOME BASE	*Hancock Park, Los Angeles*

THE ELLEMENTS OF KATE

N 2005 KATE MARA PLAYED Heath Ledger's adolescent daughter in *Brokeback Mountain*, a character who was years younger than the actress's actual age (with Ledger himself only four years her senior). Now 27, Mara still has that peaches-and-cream complexion, plus a winking, not-so-innocent sex appeal that seems to hark back to a more naive era of Hollywood. If she comes across as a nouveau Ann-Margret, she's in on the joke. Mara proudly brandishes a 1973 issue of *Playboy*—an eBay gift from her younger sister—of a girl wearing nothing but red platforms: "I've got a serious shoe thing," Mara says. "A serious *red* shoe thing."

After *Brokeback*, Mara went high adrenaline as Mark Wahlberg's love interest in the action flick *Shooter,* and dark and moody as a goth runaway opposite Woody Harrelson and Ben

Kingsley in *Transsiberian*. She played Justin Timberlake's girlfriend in *The Open Road*, snagged a small part in *Iron Man 2*, and, most recently, joined Amber Tamblyn and James Franco in Danny Boyle's first project post *Slumdog Millionaire*. The true story of a mountain climber trapped in Utah, *127 Hours* is "a dream job," says this old-school dream girl.

Redheads, Mara says, "are spicy sometimes, fiery, for sure. People think we're a little coy—but I'm totally not. Sassy? Definitely." Sassy enough to play up her auburn mane. "Oh my God, 100 percent!" she says. "That's how I pick out my clothes." She goes bold, contrasting her hair against true reds or offsetting its hue with pale pinks and teals. Her favorite shade, in fact, is one few women with her coloring would even try: "I love yellow on redheads!" she says. "Any time I wear

black or a darker color to an event, I always think, God, that doesn't do anything for me. It doesn't make me pop or stand out in any way."

Given Mara's delicate looks, the Los Angeles apartment she shares with her two Boston terriers is, at first glance, a bit perplexing: What's a girly-girl—who's certainly no pneumatic cheerleader—doing with all this football paraphernalia? "Football is a huge part of my life—*huge,*" she says. "It's not just a sport, it's family history."

Her paternal great-grandfather founded the New York Giants in 1925. His son, her grandfather, was the long-time co-owner of the team; her dad's a scout; and her uncle is now president and CEO. If that weren't enough, Mara's maternal great-grandfather founded the Pittsburgh Steelers in 1933. Thus, the memorabilia scattered around her home is studiously unbiased—as is her team loyalty. "The Giants stuff reminds me of my grandpa on my dad's side; the Steelers stuff reminds me of my mom's side," she says.

Throughout her childhood, Sunday afternoons were spent at Giants Stadium. The Giants-employed dads and uncles would watch the game from an all-business box on one side of the stadium; the Mara wives, kids, and civilian husbands took it in from their own box on the other side. It was the aunts who showed her what it means to really love football. "I grew up watching them and their reactions to the game—they're very serious about it," says Mara, laughing. "I used to think they were so nuts, but now I'm that way, too." Now, when she's on far-flung movie shoots, Mara tunes in via a gizmo that links her laptop to her TiVo back home. "Last year, I was watching football games at two o'clock in the morning in Wales," she says, laughing. "I was *not* going to miss them!"

Right: Sports mementos are scattered throughout her home. *Opposite:* Wearing Oscar de la Renta and a pair of her signature red shoes with Boston terriers Bruno and Lucius in front of her L.A. apartment building

FASHION AND ACCESSORIES

Soft shades of pink and peach offset Mara's coloring—worn together the two hues make a modern palette.

White Ray Bans make pretty pastels downtown-cool.

Wise investment: Marc Jacobs faux pearls and an Emilio Pucci shoulder bag add up to ladylike perfection.

Mara amps up eveningwear with not-so-innocent Christian Louboutin megaheels.

For running around L.A., a pair of glitzy A.P.C. flats is the perfect complement to a retro sundress.

IN FEMININE SHAPES AND SORBET COLORS, MARA'S TIMELESS CHARM SHINES.

Mara's college-sweetheart style is a perfect match for her loyalty to football and family. When the actress dons a sundress with a nipped waist or pastel, flirty shorts and tanks (she's "not really a jeans girl"), she'll make sure they're in shades that make her complexion (and, of course, her russet hair) pop in a classic, all-American way. Let other starlets grunge it up in messy eyeliner and leggings; Mara plays to her strengths, sticking to an illuminating palette and "simple but womanly" silhouettes.

❝I'M MOST COMFORTABLE IN A SUNDRESS. IT'S EASY, BECAUSE IT'S JUST ONE THING, AND YOU CAN DRESS IT UP OR MAKE IT TOTALLY CASUAL—BUT EITHER WAY YOU ALWAYS LOOK PULLED TOGETHER.❞

KATE

Easy, fresh sundresses can be found at every pricepoint, high to low, vintage to designer. This Chloé frock works for brunch with flat sandals—or a cocktail party with a strappy heel.

KEYS, WEARING A LOUIS VUITTON
JUMPSUIT, AT HER CHILDHOOD
PIANO IN HER MOTHER'S HOUSE
IN WASHINGTON HEIGHTS,
NEW YORK CITY.

Alicia

ALICIA
KEYS

EARTHY OPULENCE

OCCUPATION | _Singer, songwriter, actress_

BEST KNOWN FOR | _Lending her legendary voice to a series of soulful R&B chart-toppers_

HOME BASE | _Downtown Manhattan, New York City_

THE ELLEMENTS OF ALICIA

WHEN ALICIA Keys burst onto the scene in 2001, she was just 21, a beautiful girl in braids with a touch of urban toughness and a soulful, beyond-her-years sound. Twelve Grammys and five platinum-selling albums later (including her debut, *Songs in A Minor; The Diary of Alicia Keys; As I Am*; and, most recently, *The Element of Freedom*), Keys is hitting her stride in other arenas. She's recently engaged to her music producer fiancé, Kasseem "Swizz Beatz" Dean, and expecting her first child. So it makes perfect sense that her *ELLEments* photo shoot would take place in her mother's elegant Washington Heights brownstone—Keys, after all, has motherhood on her mind. Of her own single mom, Terri Augello, a paralegal and actress who fostered her dreams from the beginning, she says, "My mom always had a very open, positive, creative energy, because she's an actress," she says.

"Whereas other parents may be like, 'Don't waste your time. Get a real job,' she understands about art." Keys, one can only assume, will be equally supportive.

ELLE: What does your album title *The Element of Freedom* refer to?

Alicia Keys: Having the confidence to say, "This is who I am, this is what I like, this is what feels right to me—I'm sticking behind it." That's freedom.

ELLE: Do you consciously try to make records that will sell?

AK: No, that's not the place I operate from. First it's, "Is the emotion clear?" Second, "Is the melody memorable? Will I wake up tomorrow and still know it?" If it's repeating in my head while I'm sleeping, then I'm like, "Wow." Every time one of those comes, I'm surprised. It's like a gift: Oh, here, you can have this now.

ELLE: How did turning 30 feel?

AK: You start to realize that life is a multitude of things. It's partially your career; it's partially your personal life; it's partially your dreams and the things you want to achieve; it's partially your family. One without the others is not a full life.

ELLE: It's safe to say your style has evolved over time.

AK: Tremendously. [Laughs]

ELLE: Where would you say you started off?

AK: When I first started, I really wanted to be comfortable. I was basically coming straight off the streets of New York, and I was the everyday girl. Not too overtly sexy or trying too hard; I was the girl who just got up and did her thing. As I grew, I started becoming more comfortable in my femininity and trying different dresses, and I loved that, it started to become more fun, so things got a little more girly.

ELLE: Were there mistakes?

AK: Oh, jeez, that's always the most embarrassing. Over-accessorizing. At first, it was patterns, colors, braids, scarves, beads, hats—everything at once. It was fun, so why not put it all on together?

ELLE: And now?

AK: It's definitely feminine, it's tailored—high-waisted pants, sharp jackets. Jumpsuits! I like it to be strong, to have a bit of edginess. I don't like to just do the safe thing. I still like to take a chance and have some fun.

ELLE: You've always been a pants girl.

AK: At first it was because of the way that I perform, it feels good to be able to be fluid and free—you don't have to tug down on this and make sure that's covered and—'Is that okay?' As I'm playing the piano, I don't want to turn around, like, oh my goodness!

ELLE: How do you know you've found the perfect performance outfit?

AK: You can tell immediately—it changes the way you stand, the way you hold your hands, your face. You want to feel strong, powerful. It's like you're putting on your armor to go out and do what needs to get done.

Wearing an Armani snakeskin jacket

INSPIRATION BOARD

Performing in Frankfurt, Germany, May 2010

KEYS WEARS HER STATEMENT-MAKING SEPARATES WITH NEWLY ACQUIRED RESTRAINT.

Like her music, Keys' look is bold but grounded. If she's onstage performing in a wild fringe jacket, the singer will balance it with simple high-waisted trousers; or she'll let a daring jumpsuit—her favorite item—stand alone without fussy accessories (she loves the sexiness of a bare neck).

STYLE STUDY

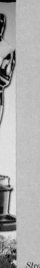

Strategically placed leather updates a simple silhouette. Her best accessory? Sheen-y, highlighted skin.

A white blouse and high-waisted pants are Keys' staples.

For a night on the town, Keys rocks a demure gown in a wild print.

FASHION FLASHBACK

The colorful tale of Keys' 2009 Oscar gown: "The dress started out as a cream color, but that washed me out, so we dyed it yellow," says Keys. "Then, on the day of the event, my stylist and I decided I should wear a color I've never worn before, so we dyed the dress deep lavender. It was very risky. The gown was disintegrating by the end of the night, but it was beautiful. I really loved it."

12. My signature scent:

Can't tell you, it's part of my Allure.

5. I feel most beautiful when:

when I am home with my hair in total Bed-head mode and eye make up smeared a bit from the night before :)

With First Lady
Michelle Obama

HER FAVORITE SHOPS

HENRI BENDEL NYC
712 Fifth Avenue
New York, NY 10019
(212) 247-1100

SHOPBOP
shopbop.com

Keys' inspirations spring
eternal: Marvin Gaye,
Stevie Wonder, Nina
Simone—"tried-and-true
people that you can listen
to without fail."

JUST **ONE** THING
AN EMBELLISHED JACKET

"I REALLY LOVE TEXTURED JACKETS THAT HAVE A TOUGHNESS TO THEM. THE RIGHT ONE CAN PULL EVERYTHING TOGETHER."

ALICIA

This Oscar de la Renta jacket is a statement unto itself. Keep the rest of the look simple, as Keys does, with tailored pants and a bare neck.

NEWTON, PHOTOGRAPHED
AT HOME IN WEST HOLLYWOOD
IN A BALMAIN DRESS.

Opposite, from top: In the Elsie Katz
Couture dress she wore to the 2008
SAG Awards; a favorite bird-shaped ring

Becki

BECKI NEWTON

SOPHISTICATED SHINE

OCCUPATION	*Actress*
BEST KNOWN FOR	*The role of fashion-obsessed Amanda on* Ugly Betty
HOME BASE	*West Hollywood, Los Angeles, and Upper West Side, New York City*

THE ELLEMENTS OF BECKI

BECKI NEWTON IS having a bit of an identity crisis. The last time we spoke, she was in full Amanda mode ("What do I wear when I want to be taken seriously? Sparkles!"), but now, a few short months after *Ugly Betty* went dark, Newton has taken on a brand-new job—and an entirely different alter ego—and is just starting to shake off the deliciously catty, fashion-possessed receptionist she played on *Betty*.

Amanda was originally conceived as a minor player on *Betty*, one of ABC's highest-rated shows for four seasons, but Newton turned her into a scene stealer—the brazenly bitchy airhead who, somewhere beneath her Versace micro-mini, hid a heart of gold (or at least gold plate). Swanning around like the world's haughtiest supermodel for four years left little time "to wander around as just Becki," says Newton. "I've either been at home sleeping or at work dressed up as a very strange character. I'm finding the middle ground to be kind of interesting."

Newton grew up on what had been her grandfather's Christmas-tree farm in Connecticut; her parents moved into a tiny cabin on the property that was supposed to be their summer home but ended up becoming the place where she and her older brother grew up. "I didn't know this world," she says, gesturing around her clothing-filled dressing room. "I didn't know what it was like to be able to go into a store and buy what you wanted. So my tastes really developed out of my imagination." Influenced by her mother, a painter, she experimented with her look, with results that were often "more Betty than Amanda," she says, laughing. "It was Betty in that I think I loved who I was. In my head, I was really stylish." Among the clothes she made for herself was a sundress cut

Cozying up in a slouchy sweater; *opposite:* Wearing husband Chris Diamantopoulos' shirt—"I love the way they smell."

"IN REAL LIFE, PLAYING DRESS-UP MEANS PLAYING MORE OF MYSELF—BEING COMFORTABLE IN CLOTHES THAT SUIT ME, RATHER THAN TRYING A DIFFERENT CHARACTER EVERY TIME I GET DRESSED."

BECKI

from thick, royal-blue wool covered in gold angels. "A totally inappropriate fabric," she laughs. "But I thought it was awesome!"

She was still shooting Olive Garden commercials when she landed the role of Amanda. (Hilariously, the OG spots aired during commercial breaks in the show's first season.) Back then, the sartorial line between work and reality was clearly delineated. "I don't

> **❝I DIDN'T KNOW WHAT IT WAS LIKE TO BE ABLE TO GO INTO A STORE AND BUY WHAT YOU WANTED. SO MY TASTES REALLY DEVELOPED OUT OF MY IMAGINATION.❞**
>
> BECKI

think I even owned high heels," says Newton. But somewhere along the way, the character began to sink her Chanel-lacquered talons into Newton's fashion sense. When Newton tried, for months, to invest in a practical black bag, she ended up coming home with the complete opposite: an oversize, silver-spangled Valentino hobo (picture a disco ball with handles).

She's taken a little of Amanda's *esprit* with her. "Yes, I love sparkly things, but now it's more about textures, layers," she says. So though the sparkly Valentino is still in rotation, these days "I'd imagine that with my husband's old gray V-neck T-shirt, skinny jeans, and cool ankle boots." But make no mistake: She may still be an aw-shucks girl at heart, but Newton's style has evolved considerably, as has her knowledge about fashion. Today, she's a front-row regular at the fashion shows of Marc Jacobs, Phillip Lim, and Brian Reyes, and fast becoming a designer favorite.

When *Betty* was canceled, Newton was promptly offered 10 new pilots, mostly variations on a now-familiar theme. "The characters were either

drunk, promiscuous, or stupid," she says. "I thought, Well, I know I can do *that*." Instead, she chose the NBC romantic comedy *Love Bites*, written by *Sex and the City* co-executive producer Cindy Chupack, which follows three loosely connected stories of love, sex, marriage, and dating. Of her character, she says, "Annie's closer to the real me, earthy, optimistic; she's like the girls in the Anthropologie catalog." But before she gets into the thick of a new show, she has other business to attend to: Soon after her *ELLEments* shoot, Newton announced she was expecting her first child with her husband, actor Chris Diamantopoulos (*24*).

They met in 2002, when he was baring it all on Broadway every night in *The Full Monty*. Fittingly, their first date sounds like a scene from a sitcom. "I was wearing this big leather jacket I'd bought for $14 at a vintage store, my hair was crazy, and I was feeling good, like '70s cool," she says. "I decided to pull my hair up and show him what a lady I was. I walked right by him in the restaurant, and he didn't recognize me!"

Opposite: In a Rag & Bone jacket ("an obsession from Fashion Week") and a sequined Christian Lacroix dress from Frock, a vintage store on New York's Lower East Side

Newton with one of her biggest sources of inspiration, her mom

With Diamantopoulos

The dining room stripes are hand painted. "It's my favorite part of the apartment—stripes in all my favorite colors."

A reminder of life back in NYC

Midcentury-inspired furnishings suit their L.A. digs.

The owl keeps the pigeons off the balcony. "My husband moves it every morning so they don't catch on."

"This is Chris' favorite picture of me because it looks like it's from the '70s."

INSPIRATION BOARD

"When you dream about special things when you're little, those things are fun and sparkly and colorful. You don't dream about black cardigans!"

FASHION FLASHBACK

Newton found these treasured party shoes on a visit to Paris during her *Ugly Betty* days, when she popped into Christian Louboutin's shop in the First Arrondissement. As she walked through the doors, she was spotted by the salesman—evidently a dedicated *Ugly Betty* fan. "He squealed, 'Amanda's here!' to the whole shop," she says, laughing. "After that, how could I leave empty-handed?"

5. I feel most beautiful when: No matter how much or how little make-up I'm wearing, I look in the mirror and see myself looking back. While I love the idea that fashion can transform you, I think you still have to look like you.

Becki

STYLE STUDY

Newton throws her biker jacket over minidresses for a look that's cool and streetwise.

Strappy metallic sandals and delicate jewelry keep the focus on a great dress.

FASHION FLASHBACK

"When I wore this sparkly jumpsuit to a major gala, I thought, Granted, I may get ripped apart [in the press], but no one will have more fun at that opera than I will!"

Horsing around with America Ferrera during a marathon Betty shoot

20. Always: have a sense of fun and adventure when it comes to fashion. Getting dressed should never feel too stressy. And take risks! The more risks you take, the braver you'll become. When in doubt, just GO FOR IT !

Backstage on Betty

Newton's mom and dad

1. My most prized possession: My mom's wedding dress. It's from the 70's, half bohemian/half victorian. She wore it in the fall of 1975 with orange and yellow chrysanthemums in her hair. I wore it to my own wedding 5 years ago and it still seemed completely modern.

6. I collect __horseshoes__ because: they remind me of my dad. He loved playing horseshoes in our backyard. Everytime I see a necklace and/or charm with one on it, I buy it. When I wear them I think of him.

HER FAVORITE SHOPS

AMERICAN RAG
*150 S. La Brea Avenue
Los Angeles, CA 90036
(323) 935-3154*

FROCK
*170 Elizabeth Street
New York, NY 10012
(212) 594-5380*

One of Newton's many eye-catching getups backstage at Betty

FASHION AND ACCESSORIES

A L'Agence biker jacket—perfectly fit to Newton's delicate proportions—works with everything from cocktail dresses to skinny jeans.

Play against type: Wear an ornate Tom Binns necklace with something low key, like a gray T-shirt.

Newton chooses fashion-forward pieces from classic brands such as Azzedine Alaïa and Chanel.

An oversize Michael Kors watch—a gift from Newton's husband to stop her from stealing his

MICHAEL KORS

NEWTON FINDS A MIDDLE GROUND BETWEEN HER FASHIONABLY AUDACIOUS PAST AND HER LOVE OF MEANINGFUL FINDS.

Newton has perfected a fashion sense that's anti-"sparkle overload" but undeniably chic. She mixes accessories that have sentimental value (her husband's oversize gold watch, a ring her father gave her) with sharp minidresses that accentuate her petite frame, an of-the-moment bag, and an embellished or patterned party shoe. Whether she's wearing a leather biker jacket over an edgy cocktail dress, or an iridescent hobo with skinny jeans and a slouchy sweater, Newton's aesthetic is all about "the cool mix."

"EVERY GIRL NEEDS A SHOE THAT GOES WITH NOTHING AND THEREFORE GOES WITH EVERYTHING."

BECKI

Newton adds a hint of shine to every ensemble. The key is to not go overboard. Choose one item with a hint of disco fever, like these festive peep-toes, and keep the rest of the ensemble matte.

BUSHNELL, PHOTOGRAPHED IN
HER GREENWICH VILLAGE HOME.

Opposite: Manolo Blahnik pumps sitting
pretty on an antique velvet chaise.

CANDACE BUSHNELL

MANHATTAN GLAM

OCCUPATION	*Novelist:* Sex and the City, Four Blondes, Trading Up, Lipstick Jungle, The Carrie Diaries
BEST KNOWN AS	*The original Carrie Bradshaw*
HOME BASE	*Greenwich Village, New York City, and Litchfield County, Connecticut*

OF COURSE, THE apartment Candace Bushnell shares with her husband, Charles Askegard—a tall, blond principle dancer for the New York City Ballet whom she married in 2002, within eight weeks of meeting—would be airy, pastel-appointed, art-lined, and located in the heart of Greenwich Village. Any of the well-heeled women who have traipsed out of Bushnell's imagination would look right at home here, lingering on her sofa or sauntering past her doorman. Even her lanky, blond Ibizan hound, Tuco, just *fits.*

It makes sense that her environment would reflect those she creates for her characters; Bushnell has made a career of detailing the lives of her own rarefied milieu, while also holding up a mirror to its values—simultaneously celebrating and skewering its various indulgences. When she was a swinging thirty-something, she fixated on a new breed of urban singleton in *Sex and the City*; through her forties, her characters grew with her in the novels *Trading Up, Lipstick Jungle, Four Blondes,* and *One Fifth Avenue* (an address which, incidentally, is a few short blocks from her own).

At 51, Bushnell has a New Yorker's grit, a sort of get-real gruffness that belies her pretty looks and her pinkish apartment. She is at her most blunt when talking about her age. "The reality is that it is true that your body shifts when you get older," she says, laughing. "Everything goes to the middle."

Now, she counteracts that slide—even if she's the only one who can see it—with clothes that have more structure, more texture; she seeks out ease, color, statement jewelry, and...sensible shoes? "When you get older you don't want to be tottering around in uncomfortable high heels," Bushnell declares. Having said that, she looks down at the 5-inch Jimmy Choos on which she is ably perched, and surveys the sea of shoes dragged out for our photo shoot—dozens of pairs that span decades of trends, not one of which could be described as 'practical'—and hoots: "I guess I just contradicted myself, huh?"

Like many of the New York-iest New Yorkers, she's a transplant. Bushnell came of age in the small, conservative town of Glastonbury, Connecticut, during the recession of the '70s, "in a family where parents said, 'We can't afford it,'" she says. "That was sort of the refrain for kids back then." She escaped conservative Rice University for New York City at 19 (she would eventually finish her degree at New York University), and promptly ditched all visible traces of her Connecticut upbringing, adopting a disco-flavored uniform primarily of stretchy Betsey Johnson tank dresses. She made the rent modeling in small fashion shows at legendary nightclubs like the Mudd Club, Xenon, and Studio 54. "In one, I wore a white dress with clear plastic cut-outs and had short punk hair, pink and green, that I'd dyed myself," says Bushnell. "I wasn't really punk...I was punk-*ish.*" Bushnell has a built-in homing device for "It"—whatever "It" happens to be; she found

Top: Tuco admires one of Tom Ford's iconic jersey dresses for Gucci. *Above and opposite:* A studded Louis Vuitton bag, rockstar heels, and Chanel jacket

❝I'M OBSESSED WITH THE IMAGE OF A WOMAN GOING SOMEWHERE—ON A PLANE, A TRAIN, HAILING A CAB. I PUT IT IN A LOT OF MY BOOKS.❞

CANDACE

herself part of an "experimental underground fashion" tribe that was "very, very New York: people who felt they didn't fit in the small towns or boroughs and had come to the city."

By her thirties, she was one of Manhattan's great media party animals, photographed out on the town, blond and impossibly slim, cocktail and cigarette in hand, cackling with '80s zeitgeist chroniclers like Jay McInerney and Bret Easton Ellis. In 1994 she joined their ranks with a *New York Observer* column called "Sex and the City," missives from the nightlife front in which her stiletto-clad alter ego, Carrie Bradshaw, dated and got dumped by "Mr. Big" (based on Bushnell's then lover, publishing bigwig Ron Galotti), and coined a new vocabulary: "absofuckinglutely," "modelizers," "toxic bachelors."

She was among the first to recognize—and embody—a new elite: childless, working women with disposable income. Back then, "it was like, 'What is this? There must be something really wrong with them,'" says Bushnell. "But then I looked around and realized every woman I knew was single." They were unapologetically self-centered, and, raised in the sexual-liberation era of the '60s and '70s, unencumbered by moral hangups (at least the way she wrote it, they were). And they had a distinct look, courtesy of young Turks like Tom Ford and Dolce & Gabbana, who were replacing '80s decadence with sleek velvet jeans and body-skimming jersey gowns. (Bushnell dug hers out of storage for our photo shoot.) The look was "young and sexy," she says. "It made women feel adventurous."

Bushnell may have been the jumping-off point for Sarah Jessica Parker's character on *Sex and the City* (even Carrie's pink sapphire ring was a replica of one Bushnell's grandmother had given her) but she insists that, on the whole, her characters aren't the fashion-obsessed lot most people assume. "That is really a misperception," she says. "It's kind of a funny thing that women do, the shopping thing. I have never quite reconciled with it. I am always like, 'Do you really need that?'" Her touchstones are *Middlemarch*, *Anna Karenina*, *Madame Bovary*, books she reads and re-reads, in which "clothing is always described, it's always part of the story, part of the characters—it's costumes," she says. She sites Winnie Dieke in her book *Four Blondes*, whose colleagues think the website they're creating should be about shopping and shoes. "Winnie's thinking, 'Is this all we think about—*shopping*?'" says Bushnell. "She's disturbed by it."

But the book she most identifies with at the moment is *Lipstick Jungle*, a tale of three busy New Yorkers juggling career and family. One, Victory Ford, is a fashion designer whose collection has bombed, "and she has to emotionally and psychologically and financially and creatively pull herself back together," says Bushnell. "These are the kinds of women that I'm really interested in: someone who is an artist but also a businesswoman, and knows how to make a deal."

Today, in many ways, she has come full circle: She and Askegard have a weekend retreat in Litchfield County, Connecticut, where she holes up "in jeans and ponytails" when her deadlines roll in. This, in fact, may be where her reality differs most from her characters' glossy fiction: Bushnell still toils away, day in and day out, on the same small writer's desk she picked up in a junk shop 20 years ago. "For me, my number-one passion has always been writing," she says. "Fashion is fun, but it's the icing."

Bushnell wears Roberto Cavalli in front of a painting by Gary Komarin.

INSPIRATION BOARD

On their wedding day in 2002, on Nantucket

"When I first came to New York in the '70s, I came from a small town and I wore argyle sweaters."

AS A SEASONED NEW YORKER WITH A FASHIONABLE PAST, BUSHNELL KNOWS HER LOOK.

Chronicling the Manhattan high life for three decades has offered Bushnell a prime seat on fashion's front lines. And she's tried it all: the late-'70s punk underground club scene, the decadence of the late '80s and '90s, and, more recently, as a polished Greenwich Village book author. Although she still has iconic pieces from her past—a lime-green Michael Kors lampshade dress, a Claude Montana pantsuit, Tom Ford for Gucci velvet pants—Bushnell has pared down her retail habits (besides the odd necessity—say, Chanel boots). "If I buy something," she says, "I really want it to be special to me."

FASHION FLASHBACK

These patent leather boots were her very first pair of Manolos: "A fashion editor friend made me buy these. She was like, 'Darling, those boots are going to change your life.' I guess she was right."

STYLE STUDY

A slinky to-the-floor evening dress in a buff hue is classic Bushnell.

Casually chic but red-carpet right in a blouse, vest, and slouchy pants.

Currently, Bushnell favors structured cocktail numbers for social events.

Husband Charles Askegard's ballet shoes

Modeling at runway shows at Studio 54 and the Mudd Club, "I was punk-ish, but I wasn't really punk."

HER FAVORITE SHOPS

CHANEL
737 Madison Avenue
New York, NY 10065
(212) 535-5505

MANOLO BLAHNIK
31 West 54th Street
New York, NY 10019
(212) 582-3007

DOLCE & GABBANA
825 Madison Avenue
New York, NY 10065
(212) 249-4100

OSCAR DE LA RENTA
772 Madison Avenue
New York, NY 10065
(212) 288-5810

"EVERY GIRL NEEDS ONE GOOD DRESS, ONE GOOD COAT, ONE GOOD PAIR OF SHOES, AND ONE GOOD BAG.**"**

CANDACE

Although she's most famous for her shoes (real and fictional), Bushnell knows that a versatile power bag like this Yves Saint Laurent can offset a whole closet-ful of fancy footwear. Besides, she says, "I don't want to change my bag every day. It's not practical." Save up for a special tote (whatever your price range), and you'll have it forever.

ever:

count yourself out.

BRYANT, PHOTOGRAPHED
OUTSIDE HER HOME IN
SILVER LAKE, WEARING
A VINTAGE GOWN.

Opposite: **Sketches from** *Mad Men*

Janie

JANIE BRYANT

RETRO ROMANTIC

OCCUPATION	*Costume designer*
BEST KNOWN FOR	*Perfectly completing the mise-en-scène of shows like* Mad Men *and* Deadwood
HOME BASE	*Silver Lake, Los Angeles*

THE ELLEMENTS OF JANIE

> **"I LOVE ALL THE DIFFERENT CUSTOMS OF DIFFERENT FASHION PERIODS—HOW PEOPLE LIVED, WHAT MOTIVATED THEM, HOW THEY'D DRESS."**
>
> JANIE

ET IN A JFK-ERA Madison Avenue advertising agency, *Mad Men* is a brilliantly orchestrated peek into the darkness that often belies bright-and-shiny perfection. The fact that you could watch the show on mute and still have plenty of subversion to dissect the next day? That's a testament to the talent of Janie Bryant. She took home a 2005 Emmy for the circa-1870s costumes of HBO's Wild West period drama *Deadwood*, but it wasn't until *Mad Men* touched down in 2007—creating ladylike, vaguely retro ripples on fashion runways from New York to Milan—that Bryant became one of the most name-checked costume designers in Hollywood.

Bryant's weakness for feminine impracticality—vintage furs, ball gowns, crystal-studded froth—may be at odds with Los Angeles' jeans-and-tee culture, but it reflects a thread of genteel Southern romanticism. When she was growing up in Cleveland, Tennessee, her mother took her to old movies, rolled Janie's ringlets on old-school foam rollers, and set an example of proper dressing. (In fact, Bryant has given her mother's dresses and grandmother's matching homemade aprons cameos on the show.)

Though the female characters' ensembles are certainly swoon-worthy, Bryant's genius is most evident in the show's menswear, where viewers have to look a little harder—and *Mad Men* fanatics mine each frame—to tease out the message embedded in every detail. Elusive, tortured lady-killer Don Draper is smooth and inscrutable in sleek, narrow gray suits; Pete Campbell, the office's erstwhile upstart, wears bright blue sharkskin that somehow betrays both his youth and his straining ambition; Roger Sterling, the martini-swilling elder statesman, is faithful to three-piece suits and collar-bar tie pins—a reminder that he's a throwback to a quickly fading past. "It's all pretty obsessive," admits Bryant with a laugh. "But every layer counts."

ELLE: So how did you end up with one of the most enviable jobs in Hollywood?

Janie Bryant: At first I was planning on being a famous fashion designer—done! Then I moved to New York and met a lot of film people. I had always, always been obsessed with old movies, and my fashion designs were always heavily influenced by different periods. I said to myself, "I love movies, I love fashion—I'm going to be a costume designer!" I really had no experience, so there were no limitations, no bound-

At home in Cleveland, Tennessee, with her sister, Laura (far left), and baby brother, Paul

At 17, attending the winter dance of a local military academy with her high school boyfriend

aries. I never even thought that way, you know?

ELLE: What were those movies you'd grown up loving?

JB: Oh, *The Wizard of Oz, Gone with the Wind, Wuthering Heights, Guys and Dolls, The Ten Commandments*—I mean, I wouldn't leave the house. I was just glued to that television! My mother really got me started; she'd take us to the Tivoli Theatre in Chattanooga, where they played the classics. I loved all the different colors, whether a fabric glittered or the skirt moved while Fred and Ginger were dancing.

ELLE: How do you get into the mind-set of a character?

JB: I love all the customs of different periods, how people lived, whether they're rich or poor, opulent or minimal—if they're foreign, say, or trying to disguise their personality. Figuring out how all those pieces are going to fit together is almost like choreographing a dance.

ELLE: Betty Draper's starchy sundresses seem to epitomize the phrase "butter wouldn't melt."

JB: Her character is incredibly shallow, but she's also very complicated. I love Betty. I probably have the most compassion for her. She had the potential of this amazing modeling career and gave it up, because that's what she was supposed to do as a woman in that period. She's always trying to create this imagery of perfection.

ELLE: You've said that her look is partly inspired by your grandmother.

JB: True. She always looked so perfectly together—the hair and the makeup and the outfits, everything matching and everything in its place in her house. On Saturdays, I loved to go with her to get her hair set. Every time my mother came back to pick me up, she was in shock at the crazy hairdo those Southern hairdressers had given me!

ELLE: I also heard that you change your own clothes multiple times a day.

JB: Since I was a child, I've always had what I call "outfit anxiety." I'll throw on a new blouse or change my accessories throughout the day. I basically keep a whole closet at work.

ELLE: Does that closet bear any traces of *Mad Men*?

JB: In the beginning it was a lot of '60s necklaces and brooches—lots of beads and crystals—and sheath dresses. That quickly passed. Then I was really into the hats and leather jackets of the '70s. Now I'm cultivating a new look with lots of '30s and '40s influences. I have this amazing little hot-pink satin quilted jacket, which is probably from the late '30s, because that was the beginning of the early, early peplum. It's a true passion for me.

ELLE: What would the costumes look like for *The Life and Times of Janie Bryant*?

JB: Well, I do feel most comfortable in an evening gown. It's my true Southern belle-ness; I can't escape it. I always tell my mother I was born with high heels on.

ELLE: You can't wear a gown to everything.

JB: That's my fantasy, for sure. But sometimes I have to be at set at 5:30 A.M., so my uniform is skinny jeans and a T-shirt, and I'll throw on some kind of leather jacket to be presentable. I always try to incorporate something a little, I don't want to say *wacky*...unique. I love anything that's shiny. Even my work boots have big Swarovski-crystal buckles.

In a '30s garden party dress with her standard poodle, Lucie: "I love the Romantic period, the Regency period–Napoleon and Josephine–all the way up to contemporary fashion."

Bias-cut '30s gowns, frothy '50s prom dresses, and '70s polyester vie for space.

Bryant's home office, stuffed with vintage magazines, modern tear sheets, and her latest assortment of hats

Bryant has scored an Emmy for HBO's *Deadwood* and two Costume Designers Guild Awards for her work on *Mad Men.*

from every
t the ready

"In my designs, I always have to feel there's an element of romance."

INSPIRATION BOARD

Inspiration: A Mad Men-era cookbook from Bryant's office

Good Housekeeping Party Book

"On Easter Sunday, my mother always dressed my sister and me in matching outfits, from our hair ribbons down to our Maryjanes."

Early influences: The Wizard of Oz, Guys and Dolls, Fred and Ginger—"I'd watch to see how the skirt moved while Fred and Ginger were dancing."

WHETHER SHE'S WEARING VINTAGE OR CONTEMPORARY, BRYANT LOVES THE ROMANCE OF A SWEEPING STATEMENT GOWN.

Both personally and professionally, clothes are Bryant's "true passion." The self-professed gown addict's taste for romance and high heels stems from her love of old movies and her upbringing in Tennessee. The costume designer is, of course, "obsessed" with vintage (she loves too many decades to choose a favorite) and can't resist hyperfeminine fabrics like chiffon, taffeta, and organza. Along with her Southern-born love for dressing up, the L.A. local finds sartorial inspiration in classic flicks like *Gone with the Wind* and *Wuthering Heights*. For Bryant, movie-going "has always been about the costume."

STYLE STUDY

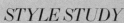

Bryant makes an entrance like Miss Scarlet in a dramatic red gown.

For a dress with a '30s feel, Bryant keeps her hair, makeup, and jewels pointedly modern.

A dress and blazer can take Bryant from the costume closet to a Hollywood party.

"Betty alone needs some 100 outfits per season; in one episode, she had 14 costume changes!" Above: Frocks for Mad Men's *Joan Holloway Harris and Betty Draper*

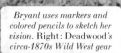

Bryant uses markers and colored pencils to sketch her vision. Right: Deadwood's circa-1870s Wild West gear

before ————————————→ *after*

❝I BUY A LOT OF '80S DRESSES AND REDESIGN THEM. I'LL MAKE ONE SHORTER, TAKE OFF THE SLEEVES, HAVE THE SIDE SEAMS TAKEN IN, AND WEAR IT WITH A GREAT, WIDE BELT.❞

— JANIE —

Altering vintage is an exercise in creative thinking. If you find a dress with a print you love but a shape you don't, try Bryant's suggestions for easy transformations.

GAINSBOURG,
PHOTOGRAPHED
IN HER PARIS HOME.

Opposite from left: Backstage at
the Casino de Paris in 1985 at
14 with her legendary parents,
Jane Birkin and Serge Gainsbourg;
her 2010 album, *IRM*

charlotte gainsbourg

CHARLOTTE GAINSBOURG

UTILITARIAN CHIC

OCCUPATION	*Actress, singer*
BEST KNOWN FOR	*Roles in indie-leaning films such as* Antichrist, The Science of Sleep, I'm Not There
HOME BASE	*Paris, France*

THE ELLEMENTS OF CHARLOTTE

T'S HARD TO FIND an American equivalent to the position Charlotte Gainsbourg holds in France. Her father, pop star Serge Gainsbourg, was the country's unofficial poet laureate (and beloved provocateur) from the '60s til the '80s; her mother, willowy English actress and sometime singer Jane Birkin, had the face—and bangs—of a generation. Charlotte, with her coltish looks, effortless style, and indie acting chops, was simply born to be, as the French would say, *supehr*-cool.

At 39, she retains a cloud of mystery, otherness; she has a charm that can't be pinpointed, the embodiment of that overused phrase *je ne sais quoi*. "It's a weird thing—being a bit shy, a bit uneasy about self-confidence and all of

In the uniform she wears to perform her record *IRM* onstage: A Balenciaga jacket, a simple tee, and jeans; *opposite:* In another Balenciaga coat. "Nicolas has done quite a lot for me."

films that challenge perceptions, like *The Science of Sleep, 21 Grams, I'm Not There,* and Lars von Trier's controversial *Antichrist* (for which she won a 2009 Best Actress award at Cannes).

Risk-taking is, after all, a Gainsbourg family tradition. When Charlotte was only 13, her career began in infamy, with "Lemon Incest," a dicey duet penned by her father about an impossible—and arguably indecent—love; the single was banned by the BBC. It took two decades for her to return to music; on 2006's *5:55* her breathy, understated vocals vaguely echo Birkin's on the infamous 1969 rendition of "Je t'aime...moi non plus." More recently on *IRM,* Gainsbourg's own distinctly hip modernity shines through.

Her work has been aided by her lineage, yes, but also hampered by it. Music, in particular, has been "terribly difficult—aspiring to do something myself while having always my father's references in my head." Gainsbourg wants to write her own songs but is haunted by his lyrics; for now, she collaborates with other songwriters and sings in English—the language is less loaded for her than French. But her attitude about all this—the shyness, the difficulties of having superstar parents—is frank, gently ironic, never self-pitying. "I have never felt that I earned what I have. I'll feel that way always—it doesn't bother me that much now, because I can just admit that I am a fraud," she says, with a wry chuckle.

Gainsbourg has constructed what she calls a "very, very quiet" life for herself in Paris with her longtime partner, actor and director Yvan Attal, and their two children, 13-year-old Ben and 7-year-old Alice. The couple met 20 years ago on the film *Aux yeux du monde,* when Gainsbourg was only 19; like her parents, they've resisted marriage. "I never liked the idea. It doesn't suit me,"

that, and still wanting to be onscreen," says Gainsbourg in her soft English-schoolgirl diction. "I like the intensity of the work. And then everything that comes after is difficult." On-screen, she is anything but reticent; she makes emotionally draining and visually surreal

she says. "I feel very superstitious that everything would go wrong as soon as we got married. It's been good this way—I want it to continue."

Surprisingly, for a woman who shies away from the spotlight, Gainsbourg's quirky career and odd, haunting beauty—a blend of her mother's eternal girlishness and her father's somewhat morose sleepiness—have made her a fashion muse to indie-leaning women around the globe, as well as to Balenciaga's Nicolas Ghesquière, whose clothes she has worn regularly since 2001. "I would trust Nicolas with my eyes closed," she says. "Even the things I don't like, I know that he's right—that in six months I'll want them. He's always a little ahead of me."

Her public wardrobe is bold and intellectual and contrasts coolly with her mussed hair and barely detectable makeup. The clothes are sexy, but in a way that appeals mostly to fellow women. It's a high-fashion armor that not everyone "gets"; like her films, her wardrobe makes a statement but also, perhaps, keeps the world at a distance. But when she's off-duty, Gainsbourg's style bears a surprising side effect of her unorthodox upbringing. "My parents gave me this idea that you sort of find a uniform that fits you and feels comfortable," she says—once you find it, you stick with it for years. Serge's uniform, influenced by Birkin's bohemian stylings, famously consisted of denim bell-bottoms and pristine white Repetto jazz shoes. (Birkin found them when he demanded footwear that was as comfortable as socks.) "I had a feeling that these clothes were like

the...*carapace*"—she struggles to find the English word—"what tortoises have on their back?" That shell was, to her, inextricable from the man himself. Likewise, though Birkin is widely remembered as a hippie clotheshorse, she too settled on a jeans-and-T-shirt uniform (a style light-years away from the Hermès status bag that was named after her in 1984) and rarely strayed.

"It's easy for me to put on the same clothes over and over again," says Gainsbourg. "I don't want to make an effort. There are some things that work on me and many things that don't, so I'm just trying to find the easy way out." For many years, she was rarely spotted without her Burberry trench—"It was so helpful, because you felt completely hidden and it was so easy to wear"—but now it's T-shirts, Notify jeans, and her beloved *bottines*: a series of identical pairs of cowboy-style booties that she had copied from an original pair of her mother's. She's worn them "every day" for five years. "I might change," she says unconvincingly. "Nicolas can't stand them!"

On her musical influences: "Dylan and Pink Floyd and Bowie and Lou Reed—I tend to come back to what I've always listened to." *Above:* Birkin and Gainsbourg with baby Charlotte in 1971

❝MY PARENTS GAVE ME THIS IDEA THAT YOU SORT OF FIND A UNIFORM THAT FITS YOU AND FEELS COMFORTABLE.**❞**

CHARLOTTE

"IT'S A WEIRD THING—BEING A BIT SHY, A BIT UNEASY ABOUT SELF-CONFIDENCE, BUT WANTING TO BE ONSCREEN."

CHARLOTTE

1. My most prized possession: *my father's black leather briefcase — with all his stuff inside... diary, glasses, check book, pictures, lyric ideas...*

17. My secret weapon: *faked calm*

STYLE STUDY

Gainsbourg shows off her smarts—not her skin—in a long-sleeve sheath.

Seen here with Ghesquière, she offsets the elegance of a feminine shaped dress with clunky shoes.

A memorable coat dresses up her jeans-and-boots basics.

FASHION FLASHBACK

Balenciaga's Nicolas Ghesquière bolsters Gainsbourg's red-carpet confidence. "I don't know what Nicolas finds in me, but I know what I find in him," says Gainsbourg, who wore an entire wardrobe overseen by the designer when she was a jury member of the Cannes Film Festival in 2001. Wearing one suit in particular, she recalls, "I felt like a little soldier. In that kind of atmosphere, where you're looked at every second, it was a great help."

10. I wish I could change my: *bosom, nose, lips*

11. I'd never change my: *bosom, nose, lips.*

6. I collect *many things* because: *I collect many things / And keep them close to me / To the ceiling / from the floor / I'm tripping on them constantly ... (La Collectionneuse / Black).*

Above: *A picture drawn by Gainsbourg's daughter;* left: *an art-lined breakfast nook*

Gainsbourg's suede bottines are based on a pair originally owned by her mom. "I always have the same boots. It's something that reassures me."

FASHION AND ACCESSORIES

Sometimes, even ultraconservative classics can be rebellious: A double-breasted blazer and turtleneck are a perfect foil for indie attitude.

Forever fresh: A slightly naive Yves Saint Laurent dress shirt and sailor-shape pants

This Balenciaga dress is pure Gainsbourg: Beautiful, but far from boring.

Céline's timeless schoolgirl satchel—more low key than any flashy "It" bag

When she's not in her trademark low-profile boots, Gainsbourg opts for bold, architectural Balenciaga heels—the higher, the better.

FOLLOWING IN THE FOOTSTEPS OF HER LEGENDARY PARENTS, GAINSBOURG REINVENTS UNDERSTATED COOL.

Although Gainsbourg has pursued a life in the spotlight as an actress and a singer, she still "feels very naked in front of an audience." Her desire to fly under the radar carries over to her daily uniform, which consists of simple T-shirts, French fisherman sweaters, military-inspired blazers, straight-leg jeans, and custom-made cowboy-inspired booties. But when it's time to step onstage—whether at a music venue or on the red carpet in Cannes—Gainsbourg's wardrobe maestro and longtime confidante, Balenciaga designer Nicolas Ghesquière, steps in with an empowering ensemble to help her rise to the occasion.

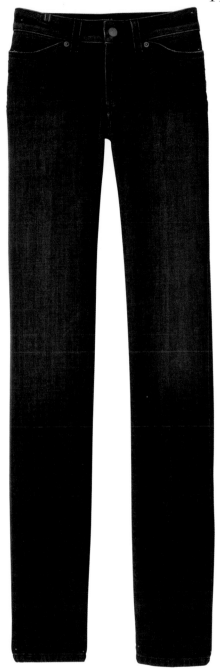

"THERE ARE SOME THINGS THAT WORK ON ME AND MANY THAT DON'T. THESE SUIT ME, AND I CAN'T CHANGE THEM."

CHARLOTTE

Gainsbourg chooses her jeans—her favorites are by Notify—based not on trends but on what works for her rangy frame, in this case boot-cut. At the denim bar of your favorite department store, keep trying different silhouettes until you arrive at one that feels "you."

ROBINSON, PHOTOGRAPHED
AT HER LOS FELIZ HOME
WEARING A TRACY REESE
DRESS SHE WORE TO THE
GOLDEN GLOBES.

Opposite: A collection of bangles
picked up on her travels

Fatima

FATIMA ROBINSON

GLOBE-TROTTER

OCCUPATION	*Choreographer*
BEST KNOWN FOR	*Crafting the smooth moves of Michael Jackson, the Black Eyed Peas, and the Backstreet Boys*
HOME BASE	*Los Feliz, Los Angeles*

THE WRITING IS ON the wall, literally, at choreographer Fatima Robinson's Los Angeles studio. DANCE HERE, it reads, and 10 young women in loose tees and baggy sweats are doing just that, stomping through a routine they'll perform onstage with the Black Eyed Peas at the Grammy Awards in two days. At the front of the room stands Robinson, arms crossed, scrutinizing every step. At 39, she has the looks of a twentysomething but the style and bearing of a relatively rare species in this town: a bona fide grown-up woman. She's wearing tailored wide-leg trousers, a starched white blouse, a menswear vest, and five-inch-long dangly earrings. The only sartorial concession to her job is a pair of brilliant yellow Nike Dunks. "I'm not a sweats kind of girl," she says. For a dance rehearsal, "I wear my jewelry, I wear my accessories, I wear my Hermès," she laughs. "I sweat in it, you know, but it's just how I am. I don't like it any other way."

You may not know Robinson's name, but chances are you've tried to emulate her signature moves. She got her big break at 21, choreographing Michael Jackson's "Remember the Time" video (a nine-minute marathon directed by John Singleton, in which Jackson romanced Iman's Nefertari) and went on to work with Mary J. Blige, Nelly Furtado, Rihanna, Snoop Dogg, Outkast's André 3000, Prince, Busta Rhymes, and the Backstreet Boys. She has also lent her moves to ads for the iPod and the Gap; directed videos for Fergie and Hilary Duff; and conceived the smooth, Motown- and disco-flavored steps of Beyoncé and Jennifer Hudson in *Dreamgirls*. Today she is back in the studio for a hot minute between creative-directing the Black Eyed Peas' world tour—overseeing everything from costumes to stage and lighting design to, of course, dance—and racing to London to lend her talents to Sade's album release. "I could be choreographing the moves for an upcoming video game one day, consulting on a commercial the next, and then doing something for the Peas the day after that," she says. "There's always something new and refreshing."

Jetting about leaves Robinson little time to luxuriate in her Spanish-style Los Feliz house, which she shares with her 10-year-old son, Xuly (who, on the day of our shoot, arrived home from school looking just as hip as Mom, with skinny fluorescent suspenders dangling from his red jeans). Decor is Robinson's other passion, and her home is infused with a luxe, comfortable warmth and a distinct coolness: deep-blue velvet couches, walls lined with art by Todd Murphy and Radcliffe Bailey, and all manner of treasures picked up on her travels. A nomad and shopper extraordinaire, she has filled her house, and closet, with finds from Japan, London, Milan, and every little town she's passed along the way. "A lot of young dancers eat McDonald's and never really leave the hotel when they're on tour," she says. "I was always the one getting out and exploring. Even if I couldn't afford anything, I'd still go into stores and feel the fabric, look at the texture."

Her mom, Khadijah Furqan, a hairdresser who was on hand to style Robinson's hair for these pages, shakes her head and laughs. "When we went to India, Fatima sent me back with so much luggage that the customs officer accused me of opening a store," she

❝I'VE BEEN TO PARTIES WHERE PEOPLE ARE LIKE, 'OH, MY GOD, THAT DRESS IS AMAZING!' I'M LIKE, 'FIVE DOLLARS AT THE FLEA MARKET.'❞

FATIMA

Left: Robinson in her mint-condition, circa-1930s bathroom; *opposite:* A vintage white dress worn with layers of jewelry and a jaunty hat

Coco Chanel, Josephine Baker, Nina Simone, Frida Kahlo. A sucker for Hermès riding boots, Goyard bags, and Vivienne Westwood's mash-up of patterns and shapely tailoring, she also owns heaps of vintage hats, gloves, and jewels. "I love that daintiness," she says. Elegance doesn't have to come with a haute price tag. The Stella McCartney-lookalike trousers she wore at the Grammys rehearsal were $2.99 at a Goodwill in Oklahoma. And even if she comes home empty-handed (which is rare), a trip to Tokyo's La Forêt mall—crowded with trend-obsessed Harajuku girls—is worth the trip, "just to see how the young girls out there are wearing their socks with their heels, how they're doing their hair," she says. "I kind of suck up the culture."

On tour with her superstar clientele, she organizes shopping days in off-the-beaten-track boutiques and occasionally even arranges for new designers she's discovered to bring their wares to a celeb's hotel room. And her own wardrobe has a viral effect: If she's got new suede architectural-heeled Martin Margiela boots, chances are Fergie will be sporting the same ones next week. "I try to inspire," she says. "And I love thinking ahead, thinking about what's next. Sometimes I have to sit down and try to enjoy being in the moment."

laughs, pointing toward a not-small rustic wooden rack she lugged back home to house the dozens of bangles Robinson procured on that adventure (plus what must be hundreds of other bracelets of all descriptions—wooden, carved, bone, painted). Even her shoes live better than most struggling young dancers: Prized pairs of YSLs and Fendis sit pretty on little footstools and tuffets, which she finds at flea markets and re-covers in lush, velvety fabrics.

Robinson was born in Little Rock, Arkansas, and moved to Los Angeles with her family when she was four. "We lived in apartments pretty much all our life and moved around a lot," she says. "I guess as a kid, I always dreamed of how I wanted to live." Never formally trained, she grew up memorizing the moves from *Flashdance*, *Dance Fever*, and *Solid Gold*, devising routines for herself and her two younger sisters to perform whenever her mother had company over, never dreaming she was paving the way toward a career. "For me, dance was just something that

I loved, never a paid thing that I aspired to do for a living," she says. She got her start in the L.A. hip-hop scene working with artists like Tupac Shakur and Dr. Dre; stylewise, though, she left that world long ago. "When it was the 'in' thing in fashion, yeah, we did the baggy jeans with the big shoelaces," she says. "But I never really embraced that part of hip-hop. I think that's what made people see me as more than a hip-hop choreographer."

Her choices are driven by one key rule: "When I walk into a room, I don't want to look like anyone else." She draws inspiration from the '20s and '30s, and gravitates toward "women who paved their own way"—

Above: In a sparkly Balmain shift and snakeskin platforms; *opposite:* Robinson's take on tailoring: A Vivienne Westwood jacket and vintage velvet riding helmet

With son Xuly, now 10

From left: Dreamgirls: Leslie Lewis, Arike Rice, Eboni Nichols, and Fatima

FASHION OBSESSION

Robinson's rule: never hit the road without an expandable tote. "This Goyard bag looks like a big clutch but turns into the perfect carry-on. You can go on a weekend trip carrying what looks like an envelope clutch, shop while you're there, and then throw it all in the expanded bag on the way home!" she says.

Dishing in the kitchen with her mom, Khadijah Furqan

On the set of a Sade video with her son as a baby and his father, the spoken-word poet Saul Williams

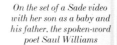

1. My most prized possession: My first thought was my son but is he a possession? He's more like a gift, my instincts, my happiness, my sanity

17. My secret weapon: *My dance moves... It seals the deal Dahling*

18. I'm obsessed with: *travelling, men w/beards, sexy underwear, Pillows, Flea markets*

5. I feel most beautiful when: *I'm naked in bed with a man. I have a LA perla mask that you hold.... It's like a lace scrim you see the world through. I feel beautiful when I'm behind it and the world looks gorgeous*

Far left: With Dr. Dre and Leslie Segar; below, from left: With Tupac Shakur; with Fergie; with Tupac Shakur; posing behind a La Perla lace scrim with friends

HER FAVORITE SHOPS

RICK OWENS
*Jardin du Palais Royal
130-133 Galerie de Valois
Paris
+33-1-40-20-42-52*

LA FORÊT
*1-11-6 Jingumae,
Shibuya-ku, Tokyo
+81-3-3475-0411*

10 CORSO COMO
*via Alessio Di
Tocqueville, 7 A
Milan
+39-02-2900-2674*

THE ROSE BOWL FLEA MARKET
*1001 Rose Bowl Drive
Pasadena, CA 91103
(323) 560-7469*

DECADES
*8214 1/2 Melrose Avenue
Los Angeles, CA 90046
(323) 655-0223*

STYLE STUDY

Robinson amps up the '40s vibe of this pencil skirt and jacket with a saucy veiled hat.

Note her mix of patterns and colors pulled together with a neutral jacket and shoes.

For a relaxed look, the choreographer opts for Balinese pants, a leather jacket, and a slouchy knit cap.

FASHION AND ACCESSORIES

A collection of costume brooches and pins make this John Galliano jacket fit for a world traveller.

Mix and match jewelry in a variety of materials—wood, beads, metal—for exotic texture.

Robinson collects dozens of hats— masculine fedoras add dash to any look, day or night.

Dress up Dolce & Gabbana pants with tough military-inspired Alexander Wang heels.

For a jet-setter on the move, a beach sarong can double as an elegant skirt—or just keep you warm on the plane.

THIS CHOREOGRAPHER MARCHES TO HER OWN BEAT WITH A CULTIVATED, ROUND-THE-WORLD SOPHISTICATION.

From her ever-expanding collection of hats to her penchant for stacks of tribal bangles, Robinson's wardrobe is a sparkling cocktail of her world travels and her Jazz Age muses. The perfect dress can make Robinson "break into poses all night." For her, that means a "long, flowing dress" for evenings out with a pair of sturdy Vivienne Westwood heels for dancing— she never hits the floor in new shoes, "no matter who designed them." When Robinson isn't practicing her moves, she's jet-setting with her superstar clients, which makes her an expert packer and, of course, a seasoned international shopper— she regularly FedExs her purchases home.

"WHETHER IT'S A HAT OR AN HERMÈS SCARF, WHAT I WEAR ON MY HEAD DICTATES THE MOOD FOR THE REST OF MY OUTFIT."

— FATIMA

Although you may not be bold enough for a hat or a turban, adopt Robinson's accessory-focused philosophy on dressing and decide the little things—shoes, jewelry—first.

MORTIMER, PHOTOGRAPHED
AT WILL ROGERS STATE BEACH.

Opposite, from left: A childhood snap
of Minnie; her daughter, Tuesday,
wakes up from a nap.

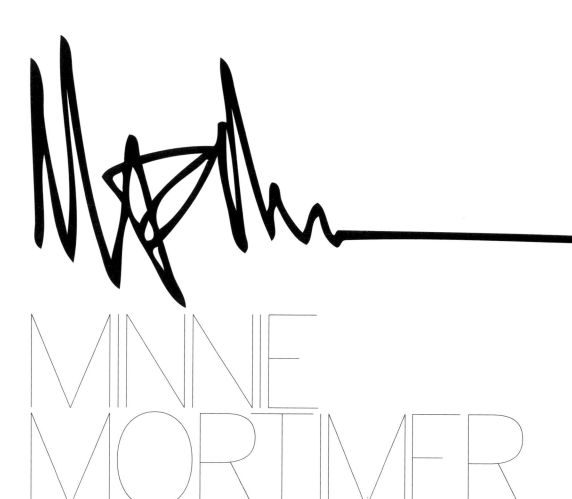

MINNIE MORTIMER

BICOASTAL COOL

OCCUPATION	*Designer of Minnie Mortimer line*
BEST KNOWN AS	*Leggy New York social fixture*
	turned Los Angeles surf mom
HOME BASE	*Mandeville Canyon, Los Angeles*

S ANY FORMER Catholic schoolgirl can tell you, spending one's adolescence in a uniform can have one of two outcomes, style-wise: Either it arrests your aesthetic, squashing it before it ever develops, or it fosters a unique kind of ingenuity in which small gestures of self-expression force their way up like weeds through pavement. Hollywood has a rich tradition of girls for whom dress-code defiance is practically a varsity sport. Remember Sarah Jessica Parker and Helen Hunt magically converting their kilts into bad-gal minis after school in the kitsch classic *Girls Just Want to Have Fun?* Or even *Gossip Girl*'s Jenny Humphrey, the current queen bee of uniform subverters, turning her bum-skimming pinafores into a look that could qualify as fetish-wear, thanks to the addition of fishnets, studs, and goth-y chokers.

Minnie Mortimer, a daughter of the Standard Oil clan and little sister of Topper (ex-husband of omnisocialite Tinsley), attended the storied Upper East Side institutions Brearley and Sacred Heart, where, she says, "I did everything I could" to bend the wardrobe rules: She lined her blazers and changed their buttons, darted and abbreviated her skirts, and switched out her regulation shoelaces. "Eventually, if you messed with your skirt too much, they'd make you put on this really awful spare that they kept in the office, which hit just below the knee," Mortimer says. "It was like wearing a dunce hat all day. To be restyled by a nun? That's a punishment."

Growing up on the Upper East Side, where "everything's navy and gray and white and charcoal," Mortimer dreamed of laid-back, colorful California. Now 29, she lives with her husband of three years, screenwriter and director Stephen Gaghan (*Traffic, Syriana*), and their 18-month-old daughter, Tuesday, in a gated mansion in Mandeville Canyon. Still, she's remained adamantly bicoastal. "I'm never going to choose," she says. "I'm a

Garden party: At home overlooking the L.A. skyline; *opposite:* In a dress that was a gift from family friend Oscar de la Renta

New Yorker at heart, but L.A.'s where I fell in love; it's where I had my baby; it's where I started my business. I feel like, if you want to get something new done, L.A. is a great place to do it."

Her day-to-day lifestyle could make any desk-bound New Yorker hang up her high heels: "I hike, I surf, I do yoga, I work, and I hang out with my baby," she says. Their backyard overlooks the city, with the tiniest sliver of coastline visible on the horizon. And Mortimer, who has a pink-and-white shortboard that was custom-shaped for her in France, has become "totally addicted to surfing." However, their current abode isn't quite as convenient for that as their former home was: "In Malibu, you just look out the window. If the waves are good, you get up early. If not, you just roll back over and sleep another couple of hours."

Their new house has a library-slash-dining room (Gaghan's Oscar for *Traffic*

THE ELLEMENTS OF MINNIE

❝WHEN I WAKE UP IN THE MORNING AND I WANT TO WEAR SOMETHING I DON'T ALREADY HAVE, I MAKE IT.❞

MINNIE

gleams among its books), a pool, and a screening room, but the thing that really cinched the deal was the closets. Gaghan, who is long-limbed and boyish, with rumpled, graying hair, laughs as he tells their house-shopping story. Mortimer arrived before him to meet the realtor and was already up in the closet—bigger than many New York studios and, under his wife's discerning eye, kept as rigorously organized as a boutique—when he showed up. "By the time I got up there, I knew we were done for," Gaghan says. "It was like, Where do I sign?"

At 13 and 14, Mortimer was escaping down to St. Mark's Place in the East Village, where the denizens were pierced, tattooed, and gender-bent. She blew her allowance on "bell-bottoms and these retro hippie flower things," lots of Day-Glo, garish plastic accessories, and, once, a treasured quilted motorcycle jacket. Her parents balked, so—like any resourceful teen—she learned to change clothes after she left the house.

That rebellious streak isn't entirely gone. Gaghan, who's on the board of *The Paris Review*, travels in intellectual circles that aren't, perhaps, entirely accustomed to his wife's fashion sense (or her Gisele-like figure). She remembers their second date, when he was doing research for a movie and brought her to a meeting. "I can't remember the name of the organization, something like the Communist Public School Teachers of

New York. And I'm in Hermès riding boots and short-shorts," she says. "Everyone was like, 'Get her out of here!' But I never really care that much. I like wearing what's fun and feels good."

Ironically—but not that unusual for a girl who grew up bucking the dress code—Mortimer has in some ways reverted back to her prepster roots. In 2009 she launched a self-titled capsule clothing collection that centered around one key basic that can be found in every Upper East Side wardrobe: the crisp and casual cotton shirtdress. With details inspired by her husband's custom-made shirts, Mortimer's frocks were named after her girlfriends: Devon, Tatiana, Tinsley (names probably familiar to social-column readers). The appeal for Mortimer was the shirtdress's versatility. "You can make it superpreppy with ballet flats and a little belt, or you can wear it with motorcycle boots—anyone can make it into whatever they want," she says. "It's a blank canvas."

The collection has grown to include flesh-tone silky tops "that feel like a T-shirt but aren't" and the "Zoe," a deceptively simple striped T-shirt dress—a just slightly longer version of the classic French bateau—that sold out after Drew Barrymore wore her black-and-white version on *Saturday Night Live*. "I design what I want to wear; that's the best motivator," Mortimer says. "When I wake up in the morning and I want to wear something I don't already have, I make it."

From left: Gaghan's Oscar for *Traffic*, discreetly tucked away; Mortimer in one of her own best-sellers, a classic striped T-shirt dress; left-coast evening wear at an East Coast affair

Mortimer in her own
design and roller skates
left over from Halloween

Fresh from a dip in the pool;
right and below: Mortimer's
rigorously organized closet

Fit for a queen: The
closet that cinched
the deal while
house-shopping

Gaghan and Mortimer snuggle up in their screening room.

FASHION AND ACCESSORIES

Studs elevate a low-profile Balenciaga sandal— perfect with tiny beach dresses or cropped jeans.

Lisa Marie Fernandez's suits function as well as they flirt.

East Coast, personified: A Brooks Brothers blazer with nautical gold buttons

A tough belt gives a demure dress personality.

For the beach, a Jack Spade canvas tote; for the city, a classic Hermès clutch

For a relaxed California look, try a holey pair of Current Elliot jeans.

MORTIMER COMBINES EAST COAST POLISH WITH WEST COAST COOL.

Splitting one's time between two coasts has its advantages: multiple wardrobes! When Mortimer hits the beach with her board, she needs little more than a string bikini and her wetsuit. If she's attending, say, a post-Oscars party with her husband, she might slip into a colorful micromini evening gown and strappy ice-pick stilettos, her hair in its signature cascading wave. But when she returns to Manhattan, she gets a case of "nostalgia for her preppy roots," which translates to a blazer and Levi's by day and prim, wasp-waisted dresses by night from old-guard designers like Mortimer's family friend, Carolina Herrera.

66AFTER I SURF, I WANT TO WEAR SOMETHING LOOSE, EASY, AND COMFORTABLE.99

MINNIE

Every blue-blooded beach babe needs a crisp cover-up—especially when it's from Mortimer's own line of pitch-perfect shirtdresses—with Etro bikini strings peeking out from the collar. Think of the swimsuit top as a new way to accessorize any warm-weather shift, whether you've played in the waves or not.

RAMPLING, PHOTOGRAPHED
AT HER HOME IN PARIS,
WEARING A LEATHER
TAILCOAT BY ANN
DEMEULEMEESTER AND
JIL SANDER TROUSERS.

Opposite: **The actress in 1975**

CHARLOTTE RAMPLING

MINIMALIST ELEGANCE

OCCUPATION	*Actress*
BEST KNOWN FOR	*Memorable roles in* The Night Porter, The Verdict, Swimming Pool
HOME BASE	*Sixteenth Arrondissement, Paris, France*

THE ELLEMENTS OF CHARLOTTE

T'S NOT JUST HER LOOKS— the cut-glass cheekbones, the body that's somehow eternally nubile— that have made Charlotte Rampling a sex symbol into her sixties. It's her unflinching, gray-eyed stare, alternately defiant, imperious, chilly, seductive, commanding. In a word, *challenging*—an adjective Rampling uses a lot. Her roles? A concentration camp survivor reunited (sadomasochistically) with a guard who once tortured her in the 1974 film noir classic *The Night Porter*; a woman compellingly in love with a chimpanzee in 1986's *Max My Love*; a middle-aged sex tourist who goes to Haiti in search of young callboys in the 2006 indie *Heading South*—every one, challenging. Posing nude alongside photographer Juergen Teller for a 2004 Marc Jacobs ad in her

fifties? Challenging. Dressing in monastic, androgynous garb by minimalist masters like Ann Demeulemeester, Jil Sander, and Rampling's longtime friend Yohji Yamamoto? Challenging. And, like the gaze, utterly alluring.

ELLE: Many of your films have been considered shocking. Do you think of yourself as a provocateur?

Charlotte Rampling: I didn't set out to do that at all, but I wanted to show the undercurrent that lives within people— not just the fun, but what actually makes us do certain things. When I started to do entertainment-type films, I just didn't feel I was in my place. My road was to be a more tricky, more marginal one.

ELLE: Your onscreen persona is often cold, elusive. Does this reflect who you really are?

CR: No, not in real everyday life, but creative people delve into the underworld of themselves, and things come up that they're not in control of at all, and that's what you use. A painter may paint violent, bizarre pictures—he probably won't seem like that at all, but that's his shadow side, the way he needs to express himself.

ELLE: You once said that getting what one wants from men is about having a certain magnetism, and that you knew you had it.

CR: Well, it's really a preposterous statement. [Laughs]

ELLE: Yes, fabulously so.

CR: I said that when I was very young. But...if you are a really good-looking woman and you use your looks intelligently and you use your *intelligence* intelligently, men cannot, will not resist that.

ELLE: You asked our photographer specifically not to heavily retouch your photos.

CR: It's not that I like my face better with age. Not at all. I liked it better when it was younger. But whatever it looks like, I want to live with it because that's my living experience. I want to go right through to the end with that kind of attitude.

ELLE: What's your thinking about onscreen nudity?

CR: If there's nothing particularly interesting about the fact that you're naked—if you wear nakedness like you wear clothes—then there's something very, very alluring about that. A naturalness with your body and an un-complexed attitude—that is very beautiful on a woman, even if she doesn't have the so-called perfect body. Who cares about perfect bodies?

ELLE: You have done some rather interesting photo shoots with Juergen Teller.

Opposite: On the streets of Paris in Robert Clergerie loafers and a custom Driza-Bone Mackintosh from Australia. "It's an authentic trench coat they wear in the Outback—very tough leather."

With Paul Newman in Sidney Lumet's 1982 movie *The Verdict*, one of her few Hollywood films

Publicity shot from the 1974 film *The Night Porter*

CR: [In one 2009 shoot] I was naked in the Louvre, just standing there in front of the Mona Lisa and the Greek statues, using my body as if it was anything—not posing, not making any business about it, but just being there, naked.

ELLE: How did that feel?

CR: A bit cold. [Laughs] And a bit inhibited, because the pictures are all staring at you. We were two tiny bodies, the model Raquel and me, and we actually felt very amazed and powerful.

ELLE: In the '60s, you had a very exuberant, sexy look.

CR: Well, I was experimenting with all sorts of colors, styles, shapes, feels. There was such an explosion of different styles, especially in all the minidresses, the miniskirts. Everything that was "mini" I leapt into. I felt great in it. There was this incredible sense of freedom.

ELLE: When did your current look develop?

CR: Actually, through my husband [now-ex, Jean Michel Jarre], who was wearing a lot of Yohji Yamamoto's clothes. At the time, I was still just wearing odd, funny, funky things, colorful things, not a particular style—but I got very fascinated by this whole architectural style that Yohji had. It was something I went really seriously into, still am. I loved the idea of these suits that aren't cut the way Dior or Chanel would cut a suit—they're unusual, off-center, but still exquisitely tailored. It's a Yohji trouser suit—it couldn't be anyone else's. And there's no hype around Yohji. That's also what I loved, because all the fashion hype can get overpowering.

ELLE: Do you find that that kind of clothing has a certain physicality—does it make you walk or sit differently?

CR: It does. And it took quite a long time to get used to. I never saw many women doing it because it's quite a difficult way of being, actually, Yohji.

ELLE: So what's your day-to-day look?

CR: Jil Sander slacks—I love the fabric, the cut. A shirt or T-shirt, a cardigan, and a sort of soft jacket. [Yves Saint Laurent designer] Stefano Pilati gave me two beautiful men's jackets, so I wear those a lot. And I live in lace-up shoes. I've probably got 20 pairs.

ELLE: Why so masculine?

CR: I just don't seem to be able to dress in a girly way. I guess I really am an androgynous person.

ELLE: Says the sex symbol!

CR: Well I just feel that femininity is who you are. It depends on how you feel, say, when you go out in the morning. Do you need to add touches to your femininity? I don't feel that I do. But other people would probably say, "Well, oh, God. She looks a bit plain." But if that's the way I feel good, as just me, Charlotte, going out for a day, then that's fine. There's nothing else that's needed.

Above: Photographed on her couch; *opposite:* In her bedroom

❝THE INNER, UNCONSCIOUS WORLD, THE ONE WE'RE NOT DIRECTLY IN CONTACT WITH OR IN CONTROL OF—THAT'S THE ONE I TRY AND PRIVILEGE.❞

CHARLOTTE

Rampling in her sitting room in a dress by
Jean Muir that "hangs particularly well"

CHARLOTTE'S WORLD

Inspiration wall in
Rampling's living room

A portrait by her cousin,
Madeleine Rampling

Shoes by Yohji
Yamamoto, Robert
Clergerie, Jil Sander,
Fratelli Rossetti,
and Church's

The foyer of her home, which she shares with her boyfriend, Jean-Noel Tassez

Stacks of scripts and a portrait by Anthony Palliser; *below right:* Drawings of Rampling, her two sons, and her stepdaughter, all by Madeleine Rampling

INSPIRATION BOARD

The actress in 1964

The cover of "Comme Une Femme," her 2002 album

FASHION OBSESSION

Step into Rampling's simplified menswear-inspired style: "The only shoes I wear now are men's brogues," says Rampling. "I own around 20 pairs." With tuxedo pants and a blazer or bare legs and a miniskirt, these J. Crew oxfords capture Rampling's confident tomboy look in a flash.

Above and right: Charlotte Rampling in the mid-'70s. "The '70s were quite controversial, really taking the lids off a lot of taboos. A lot of powerful films were telling stories like they'd never been told before."

HER FAVORITE SHOPS

YOHJI YAMAMOTO
25 rue du Louvre
Paris, France
+33-1-45-08-82-45

JIL SANDER
56 Avenue Montaigne
Paris, France
+33-1-44-95-06-70

ROBERT CLERGERIE
5 Rue Cherche-Midi
Paris, France
+33-1-45-48-75-47

YVES SAINT LAURENT
6 Place Saint-Sulpice
Paris, France
+33-1-43-29-43-00

STYLE STUDY

For formal events, Rampling often chooses clean, tailored suits over gowns.

Sly armhole cutouts give this classic jacket a bit of an edge.

A plunging neckline gives this otherwise austere gown Rampling's signature sex appeal.

Milla

MILLA
JOVOVICH

FREE SPIRIT

OCCUPATION   *Model, actress, singer, designer*
BEST KNOWN AS   *Supermodel turned action heroine*
HOME BASE   *Beverly Hills*

THE **ELLE**MENTS OF **MILLA**

> **"I'M VERY MUCH INTO DRESSING UP, AND MAKING MOVIES IS A REALLY WONDERFUL EXTENSION OF THAT— OF ME LOVING TO TAKE ON DIFFERENT CHARACTERS AND LIVE A BIT LIKE A KID."**
>
> MILLA

W HEN I WAS A kid, I was always trying to find a little doorway that would take me into wonderland," says Milla Jovovich. "In a sense, I found it through my career." At 34, Jovovich has had, so far, at least four careers—model, actor, singer, designer—that, together, have spanned more than 25 years, each of them highly influenced by something she has in large supply: whimsy.

At age six, Jovovich moved from the Soviet Union to London before settling in Los Angeles with her father, a Serbian doctor, and her mother, a Russian former actress. After moving to the U.S., her parents split and she was raised by her mother; before she even hit adolescence she was helping support the family as a model. "We had a beat-up old Chevrolet and big dreams, and it was my responsibility to work to help my family," she says. At 11, she was pouting seductively in Revlon's "Most Unforgettable Women in the World" campaign. Herb Ritts, Richard Avedon, Peter Lindbergh—everyone wanted to shoot the blue-eyed "pretty baby," the most provocative child model

since Brooke Shields. (In fact, she would eventually retrace Shields' footsteps, starring in 1991's *Return to the Blue Lagoon*.) "That period of my life, 11 to 14, was pretty intense," she says. "Everyone was doing a little Lolita story on me." And not everyone was happy about it. A Christian group was up in arms about her pictures. "Avedon had dead baby pigs thrown at his door because of me," she says, an act presumably in protest of what some decried as child exploitation. Now, as the mother of three-year-old Ever Gabo, her daughter with her husband, director Paul W. S. Anderson, Jovovich admits she looks back and wonders. "How could people have thought I was an adult?" she says. "I looked like a child with a lot of makeup on trying to act grown up."

Much of her career has seemed to be an effort to recapture that cheated innocence. At 18, she released an album, *The Divine Comedy,* inspired, tellingly, by her love of "elves and magic trees." And in her films, she's always gone after quirky characters; unlikely roles for a woman of her obvious beauty. She chooses indie movies such as *The Messenger* and *The Million Dollar Hotel,* which "are always really crazy, dark, or really fun and interesting," but has found a more prominent niche playing

From top: Jovovich in a Temperley dress, one of her favorite labels; reading one of her treasured antique illustration books; *opposite:* Outside of L.A.'s Chateau Marmont

physically perfect, utterly fearless avengers in action movies. First, there was Leeloo, the orange-haired "perfect supreme being," who wore little more than a web of Ace bandages in *The Fifth Element*. Then came Alice, heroine of the post-apocalyptic *Resident Evil* franchise— an ass-kicker created by a man familiar with Jovovich's considerable strengths: her husband, who directed the films (Jovovich co-designs the series' costumes).

Jovovich also draws, makes music, and, of course, designs. For four years, her Jovovich-Hawk collection, created with old friend Carmen Hawk, was one of fashion's most influential young-designer collections. (The label is currently "semiretired" in order for Jovovich to get back to acting and tackle the job of mothering.) But she doesn't need an official fashion job to get her sartorial juices flowing. "Wanting to create a look or a character is a constant in my life. I like to create characters even when I'm at home," she says. "It's like, Who do I want to be today? What character do I want to put on?"

Indeed, she dresses a bit like a child who happens to have an exceedingly well-stocked costume cupboard, following her heart instead of the trends and gleefully embellishing. "My style gives people the feeling that I'm not your ordinary run-of-the-mill character—it's a little wacky; it's got a sense of humor," she says. "It's always had a little bit of irony." So, should she choose to pair "an awful, horrendous-looking '80s belt" with a beautiful, romantic Temperley dress, she's in on the joke.

Her style, she says, has mellowed slightly. "Ten years ago, I was pretty crazy. I'd wear anything—1920s underwear with high heels to a party," she says. But the "fun factor" hasn't changed. If she's feeling uninspired, she refers to her library of

rare, early-edition illustration books by artists such as Arthur Rackham and Edmund Dulac to inspire a color palette or a detail. "I have a collection of eclectic things that I like to throw in there to sort of make people smile, I guess," she says. "It's a little wink-wink." She stockpiles antique accessories, including little hats and veils, combs, hairpieces, and headbands, accumulated from swap meets and vintage stores in L.A., Paris, Barcelona, and Italy. "I'll stay up until three in the morning googling vintage hats or Victorian walking suits," she says. "You can find *anything*—just Google it."

And even when she's hanging at home with her daughter, pedestrian sweats are out of the question. She pads around in staples from American Apparel—basic tees, shorts, and tights—topped off with an interesting necklace, maybe a shawl. "It makes me feel a little bit more mysterious and a little bit more interesting," she says. "Simplicity is hard for me."

Opposite: In her day-to-day American Apparel basics, with a touch of whimsy; *from top:* The jacket of a museum-worthy Victorian walking suit; a shot of Milla at age 12 by Peter Duke

"Mystique is so important. It's that fairy dust you sprinkle around to make people believe something," says Jovovich, wearing a Kenzo dress in her screening room.

INSPIRATION BOARD

STYLE STUDY

There's an element of girlish dress-up in Jovovich's silky, ultrafemme dresses.

Fun, indeed: Layers of necklaces, a net hair ornament, and a flirty flapper-style dress

A skinny belt adds structure to a slinky, negligee-style dress.

FASHION OBSESSION

Jovovich finds style inspiration in everything from fairy tales to paintings. Here, a list of her favorite artists:

1. Eighteenth-century portrait painter Sir Thomas Lawrence
2. Seventeenth-century Baroque artist Anthony van Dyck
3. French fairy-tale illustrator Edmund Dulac
4. Irish stained-glass maker and book illustrator Harry Clarke
5. English children's book illustrator Kate Greenaway

From left: A framed fashion illustration; a card to Jovovich's daughter, Ever, from her godfather, filmmaker Wim Wenders

I've loved you with a love ever-lasting. I've called you by your name. I hold you in the palm of my hand. You are mine!

From God for Ever.

3. The sexiest thing in my closet:

ME!

13. Every woman needs a:

GBF! (gay best friend)

15. When I fell in love I was wearing:

cute undies! ~~[scribbled out]~~

always a MUST!

A shot of Jovovich at age 12

7. My lifesaving beauty product:

lipstick. you can use it on your lips, ~~cheeks~~ cheeks or eyes. it's a great quick fix when you're on the go.

10. I wish I could change my:

morning moodiness
I'm not a good morning person.

1. My most prized possession:

my daughter's bunny!
she has to sleep with it!

FASHION AND ACCESSORIES

Don't hesitate to layer eclectic statement jewelry against a multicolored print.

Not just for evening, a shimmery Oscar de la Renta vest adds an unexpected jolt to soft florals and T-shirts and jeans alike.

A feathery Balenciaga bag adds 1920s-style romance.

Juicy Couture T-straps dial down the va-va-voom in favor of a quirkier sort of sex appeal.

WHETHER SHE'S ACTING, DESIGNING, OR DRESSING, JOVOVICH IS A BORN STORYTELLER.

Jovovich has equally eclectic taste in clothes and movie projects. From her huge collection of vintage headpieces and shoes to her preference for designers, such as Alice Temperley, who share her love of whimsy and romanticism, she engages her vast imagination in dressing. Whether she's accessorizing a T-shirt and leggings from American Apparel with a shiny belt and a sparkly cloche or mixing a floor-length floral dress from Kenzo with a flapper headband, the Ukrainian-born stunner always tries to "make things special" by accenting each outfit with an unexpected twist.

66I LOVE COMBS, HAIRPIECES, AND HEADBANDS FROM THE '20S. I LIKE TO DRESS UP— I'M A REAL GIRL WHEN IT COMES TO THAT.99

MILLA

We could all learn from Jovovich's ability to have fun with her wardrobe. This embellished Jennifer Behr headband adds a touch of unpredictability to even a simple dress or a tailored jacket.

PHOTOGRAPHY CREDITS